Object Lessons that Speak Louder than Words

70 Action-based Activities that Teach

Individual Differences
Being Unique
Relating to Others
Working with Others
Setting Goals
Personal Character
Personal Choices

by Shawn Becker

Copyright @2008

Educational Media Corporation®

P.O. Box 21311

Minneapolis, MN 55421

800-966-3382 or 763-781-0088

www.*educationalmedia*.com

Library of Congress Catalog Control Number 2008922230

ISBN: 978-1-930572-53-9

Printing (Last Digit)

10 9 8 7 6 5 4 3 2 1

Production editor—

 Don L. Sorenson, Ph.D.

Graphic design—

 Earl R. Sorenson

Dedication

I would like to give thanks to the two people who first introduced me to adventure-based learning: Dr. Jeff Ashby and Dr. Don DeGraff. Their class 13 years ago opened my eyes to a whole new way of reaching people, igniting a personal and professional passion inside of me. I do not know what I would be doing now if they did not have the wisdom and courage to offer that class. I do know that I would have spent a lot less money on activity supplies over the years and would also have more storage space than I do now.

I would also like to thank my parents for always supporting me and encouraging me to do what I love doing. I have been able to take the risks I have taken because I knew they would always be there for me. I tend to wait until the last minute to finish things, even though this would frustrate my mom, but she was always there to help me out in any way I needed. She spent many hours painting or sewing new activity ideas I had.

Finally, I would like to thank my beautiful wife Kristen for all her support. She puts up with a lot, from me purchasing equipment and supplies for activities to helping me test new activity ideas. I am very grateful to have her by my side, especially when I am presenting and working with groups. She fills me with confidence and inspiration.

About the author

Shawn has over a decade of experience leading activities with groups of all ages. He has been using activities that teach with thousands of people in a variety of settings, including schools, camps, churches, businesses, and conferences. Shawn has been passionate about activity-based education/counseling since he took his first Adventure Therapy class from the University of Northern Iowa in 1995. Since then, he has also returned to the University of Northern Iowa to teach the same class that started it all for him. Shawn also started his own company in 2000 called EduVenture. EduVenture combines education with the hands on nature of adventure-based activities. The mission behind EduVenture is to help people become personally involved and connected with their learning, training, and development.

Shawn has a Masters degree in Community Counseling from the University of Northern Iowa and received his School Counseling Certification from the University of Wisconsin-Milwaukee. He is currently a School Counselor at Badger Middle School in West Bend, Wisconsin. Shawn continues to facilitate staff and leadership development workshops, facilitator trainings, youth leadership camps, family fun events, and ropes course groups.

Introduction

One of the author's greatest joys is creating a ripple effect with new activities that may never end. It is such a nice feeling to know that an activity will keep spreading and impacting countless people. Shawn has been self-diagnosed with "Activity ADD," because he is always searching for new activities that can be used to teach the same points. He also believes that people learn best by doing. This "Activity ADD" and personal philosophy led to the creation of *Object Lessons that Speak Louder than Words.*

The book is not a "sit there and listen to what I have to say" approach. Rather it is an "experience for yourself," action-based book appropriate for grades 5 and up. It will help you reach multiple levels at the same time as it taps into an individual's thoughts, feelings, and behaviors. Participants will have to think, feel, and do during the activities and discussions. These lessons can easily be woven into your existing curriculum and goals. Students will look forward to your new innovative lessons. Each object lesson is followed by a set of processing questions. It is during this discussion that the group members will transfer what they experienced and learned during the activities to their "real life" situations. Your students will be challenged to think about their relationships, emotions, goals, values, and lives. The object lessons will open doors as you help your students make meaningful connections with their physical, relational, and emotional worlds.

70 Action-based Activities that Teach

Table of Contents

Individual Differences and Being Unique

1   Different Interpretations

Topic: Respecting differences, People's perceptions

Materials: A blank piece of paper for each participant

Time: 20 minutes   ***Space:*** Classroom

Activity: This activity can provide a visual display of the unique interpretations we all have of the same information. Hand out a piece of paper to each participant. Instruct the group not to look at their neighbor's, but concentrate on their own sheet of paper, following your instructions carefully. Tell the participants to (1) fold the paper in half and tear off the upper right-hand corner, (2) fold in half again, and tear off the upper right-hand corner, (3) once more, fold in half and tear off the upper right-hand corner. (4) Unfold your paper, hold it up, and look around the room. You'll find that each participant has a different "take" on your instructions. The exercise clearly demonstrates to the participants that we do not all hear/interpret information in the same way.

Participants will ask you how to fold it. They may ask if you wanted it folded in half according to length or width. Do not answer them and just repeat the instructions over and over. You don't want to influence their perspectives and decisions.

Discussion:

1. Why don't all the pieces of paper look the same if we all followed the same directions?

2. What problems can occur if we interpret information in different ways?

3. What can we do to prevent problems with these interpretation differences?

4. At times, your coaches, teachers or parents explain things to you and have expectations. What happens when you do something different because of what you "thought" they said or wanted?

5. What difference would it make if you asked for clarification to understand exactly what they meant?

6. What could you do to make sure that everyone ends up with the same design in the end? You can visually demonstrate and have them follow you step-by-step.

2 Finding North

Topic: Respecting differences, People's perceptions

Materials: None

Time: 10-15 minutes   **Space:** Classroom

Activity: This is another quick activity to demonstrate that we all have our own unique interpretations, ideas, beliefs, values, and behaviors. Have your group spread out around the room. You want them to have enough space around them so that they can freely spin in place with their arms straight out. Tell the group that you have misplaced your compass and that you need them to help you find the right direction. Have the group members close their eyes and spin around three times in place. When they have completed their third rotation, ask them to point in the direction that is north. Make sure they still have their eyes closed!

Once they are pointing to north, have everyone open their eyes and look around without moving their arms. You will notice that there are many different ideas of where north is. You can tell them where the true north is, if you know. Or you can do what I do and randomly point, saying that it is north! You may want to give them another chance to spin and find east, west, or south. Maybe have them find north again to see if they all get it right. I bet most will not. You can vary the number of spins to add to the confusion.

Discussion:
1. What did you notice once you opened your eyes?
2. Did you want to change where you were pointing once you saw other people pointing to a different north?
3. Was anyone else pointing exactly where you were? Did that matter? Was it okay to be pointing in a direction no one else was?
4. Is it difficult to be the only person heading in a direction that is different from the rest of your friends or peers? The only person not using alcohol or drugs? The only person not cheating? The only person who doesn't lie? The only person who studies and gets good grades?
5. We all have our own beliefs, values, feelings, and choices that make us unique. Is it okay to be different from others?
6. Where do the messages that we should all think, act, and feel the same come from? (i.e., media, TV, magazines, peers)
7. What are some things about you that make you unique?

3   Drawing Perceptions

Topic: Respecting differences, People's perceptions

Materials: Pens/pencils/markers, paper

Time: 20-30 minutes   **Space:** Classroom

Activity: You can play it one of two ways: If you have a two-sided chalkboard, you have one person on one side and the other person on the other side. The facilitator describes a complete face, one section at a time, (e.g., round face, large oval eyes, hoop earrings, small ears, etc.) until the participants finish the face. When the facilitator and the participants are done with the drawing, compare the two drawings to see how each person "perceived" the description. The other way is to have the facilitator read the description and the group does it on paper. Later, everyone compares their drawings. You could use this to discuss perceptions, diversity, differences, and labels.

Discussion:

1. Does anyone have a face that is exactly like the one I drew?

2. Why does your picture look different from what I described to you?

3. We all have differences in how we perceive things. How can differences in perceptions affect our lives? Communication with parents/friends/teachers. You may have your own interpretation for an assignment or test. You may not do your chores the way your parents want you to.

4 Do Labels Always Fit?

Topic: Judging others

Materials: Cans of fruit or vegetables

Time: 20-30 minutes   **Space:** Classroom

Activity: This is a simple object lesson to discuss how we label others in addition to how unique we are inside. All you need is to take the label off a can of fruit or vegetables. You may also want to add a dent or two to the can. Put the can in the middle of the group and let the group examine it. Ask them to describe the can. Some may say that it's shiny, that it has dents, and that it has no label.

Discussion:

1. Ask the group how their descriptions of the can relate to people.

2. Dents, of course, because we aren't perfect and we all have some sort of fault.

3. Have the group share some of their faults if they are able to do this.

4. The can gives off a reflection. We reflect what people say about us. Some may say we're really good at something, while others may say we are not good. We will listen to others and let them decide what we are good or not good at. Have you ever stopped doing something you enjoy because another person said you were not good at it or should not be doing it?

5. We also have labels like the cans do. What are some of the labels that are given to people?

6. Do you think that cans ever get the wrong label put on them? Do you think that people get mislabeled?

7. Ask the group what would happen if the can was labeled with a food they did not like.

8. Have them share some of the food labels they would stay away from.

9. We often only look at the outside of people when we label and judge them. What could we be missing if we only judge people by the outside?

10. You may get a can of food that is mislabeled. It may be labeled as something you really like. You may open it up and be disappointed. You might also get a can of food that you avoid because of its label. Once you open it up, you may find that you really like it once you try it or that it was mislabeled. The same is true for people. We may find a person who has a label we like. But then when we really get to know them, we find that we really do not like them after all. We can also find that we like someone who had a label we avoided once we take the chance to get to know them.

11. Labels can be misleading and also damaging to and for people. We should avoid the labels and look on the inside for what counts because not all labels are accurate.

5   Fresh or Fake

Topic: Judging others

Materials: Fresh and artificial flowers, vases, water

Time: 20-30 minutes   **Space:** Classroom or larger space

Activity: Before class, find one artificial flower and one fresh cut flower, and place each in the vase. Fill the vase with water. (Flowers do not need to be the same type, but if they are similar, it will enhance the effect of the lesson.) You can ask the group to identify which of the flowers is fake or real just by looking at them. Have the students distinguish the real flower from the fake flower, not by sight, but by using their other senses, such as smell and touch. In a similar way, we can identify a fake individual from a genuine person. Looks may be deceiving, but there are ways to tell.

Tell the class that you have two beautiful flowers. Show them the flowers and explain that both flowers are beautiful. Ask if they can you tell any difference between the two flowers. Both flowers do look pretty. Both are sitting in water and in a vase, but one is not real. I am sure you can tell which flower is fake. Fake friends/people are a lot like this fake flower. They may say they are your friends or that they are positive people who make good choices. However, their daily walk may be fake or artificial.

Let me show you some other ways you can tell the difference between real and fake. Ask a volunteer to come forward, touch the fake flower, and describe how it feels. Then have them touch the petals of the real flower and describe how it feels. Yes, the fake flower feels stiff, but the real flower is smooth and soft. Ask another volunteer to come up and smell the fake flower and describe what he or she smells. Then have them smell the real flower and describe how it smells. The fake flower really has no scent, though it might smell like plastic. The real flower smells good. Real friends/ role models are like this real flower; not only do they look like your friends or like role models when they are around you, but they also act the same way everywhere they are.

Discussion:

1. What are some of the differences between the two flowers?
2. How were you able to tell the two of them apart?
3. Which of these flowers would you want to be?
4. Would you rather have a bunch of fake flowers or real ones in a vase?
5. What can you do to make sure that you are picking "real" flowers?
6. How can you tell the difference between a real or fake friend?
7. What are some characteristics of a true friend?
8. What are some characteristics of a true role model?
9. How can you tell the difference between a real or fake role model?
10. Who are some role models that young people look up to?
11. Who are some people students your age look up to that might not be "real" role models?

Shawn Becker

6   Dollars and Selves

Topic: Personal value

Materials: $1.00 or $20.00 bill

Time: 20-30 minutes   **Space:** Classroom

Activity: This lesson can reinforce that others will love and accept us, no matter what. Start off by showing the group your $20.00 bill. Ask if anyone in the group wants the $20.00. You will more than likely see all the hands go up in the air. You can tell the group that you will give the $20.00 to one of them, but only after you do a few things to it. The first thing you will do is crumple it up in your hands. Ask who wants it now. You should still get just as many hands in the air volunteering to take it off your hands. Then drop it on the floor and grind it with your foot. Pick it back up. Now that it is crumpled and dirty, ask if anyone wants it. Again, hands will go up.

Now the group will be ready for your lesson. Explain that no matter what you did to the $20.00 bill, they still wanted it. The bill did not lose its value even when it was crumpled and stepped on. It is still worth $20.00. Even if it is put through the washing machine, it is still worth $20.00. The same is true for us. We are all like the $20.00 bill. There are times when we are stepped on and smashed into the ground. There are times when we are crumpled and run over by our decisions and life circumstances. There are times when we feel worthless. The thing you need to keep in mind is that we never lose our value. No matter what happens to us, we are still priceless, especially to those who love us. Leave your group with the following thought: Our worth comes from who we are inside, not in what we do or who we know.

Discussion:

1. Why did people still want the money even after it was crumpled and stomped on?
2. Did the money lose its value after it was crumpled or stepped on?
3. Do people lose their value after they are stepped on?
4. Why do some people feel like they are worth "less" based on how they are treated?
5. Can you name times when people might feel worthless?
6. What things might a person your age do to deal with feelings of worthlessness?
7. What do you think people who feel unaccepted and worthless need?
8. What can our group/school do for those people?
9. What can you do for those students or individuals who feel worthless?
10. Do you always know who is feeling this way? Why or why not?
11. When you are having a bad day and feeling dejected/rejected, what do you do to feel better?
12. Do we always have control of the things that happen to us that might leave us feeling crumpled?
13. Do we have control over how we react to those things beyond our control?
14. Are we in control over whether or not we allow circumstances and people to make us feel worthless?

7   *Our Many Flavors*

Topic: Diversity, Individual differences

Materials: A large package of Jelly Belly jelly beans

Time: 30-45 minutes   **Space:** Classroom

Activity: This is a great activity to demonstrate the value in being unique and different.

Jelly Belly jelly beans work great for this activity because they come in over 40 different flavors. Each flavor has its own unique color pattern to help identify it.

Start the activity by giving every person about 5 to 10 jelly beans. Tell them to take a few minutes to look at their jelly beans. They should pay close attention to what each one looks like so they can see the variation in colors and patterns. Then they can start eating the jelly beans. Ask them to eat one at a time so they can try to identify the flavors. Give them a few minutes to eat all of their jelly beans. If someone does not like the jelly beans or cannot have them for some other reason, have them look at the ones they get. They can still talk about the colors and maybe guess the flavors.

Discussion:
1. Tell me about some of the flavors you had.
2. Were you surprised by any of the flavors?
3. Did you look at one and think that you would like it because of its color?
4. Was there one that you thought would have tasted good but turned out bad to you?
5. Were you surprised by liking one that you thought looked bad?
6. In a sense, you judged the jelly beans by how they looked. Do we do that with people?
7. What are some things on which we judge people?
8. Have you ever met someone that you thought you would not like based on how they looked?
9. Have you ever been surprised by someone once you got to know them? (Either you liked them when you did not expect to or they looked nice but were not.)
10. Do people sometimes leave us with a bad taste in our mouths, just like some of the jelly beans did?
11. What would it be like if all the jelly beans were the same color and flavor?
12. What would it be like if all people looked and acted the same?
13. What are the good parts about living in a diverse world?
14. No matter what the jelly beans looked like or tasted like, they were all the same because they were all Jelly Bellys. No matter what people look like on the outside, they are all the same and have the same feelings, goals, and needs.

Shawn Becker

8 Equal Start

Topic: Individual differences/talents

Materials: Water, buckets, cups, measuring cup

Time: 20-30 minutes   **Space:** Classroom

Activity: In this challenge, students will be trying to fill various-sized glasses with equal amounts of water. Before this activity, you'll need to fill a bucket with water. One way to do this so that the activity will work is to first fill the smallest glass with water. Then multiply the amount in that glass by the total number of glasses (participants) you will have. For example, if the smallest glass holds 1/2 cup of water and you have ten glasses, you'll need to pour five cups of water into the bucket. Give each person a glass and say: Divide up the water in the bucket so that each participant has exactly the same amount. You must use all of the water in the bucket.

When the group has finished dividing up the water, use a measuring cup to measure the amount of water in each glass. Have the students each take note of how much water is in their glass, then let them continue working to fill all the glasses equally. Measure the amount of water in the glasses as many times as participants ask you to. When students have finished dividing the water equally, say: In life, we don't all have the same advantages and challenges. Each of us is created uniquely and faces a different set of circumstances. But we all have something to offer other people. When we share the unique talents we have inside of us instead of living only for ourselves, we help make life better for others. Just as in this activity, if we refuse to share with others, everyone loses.

Discussion:

1. What were some of the challenges in this activity?

2. Was it difficult for your group to end up with equal amounts of water? What made it difficult?

3. What are some different situations people might be born into?

4. Who are some people who have overcome adversity to accomplish something great?

5. What are some unique talents you have that you can offer this group/classroom?

6. Why is it a positive thing that we all are not born into the same situation or have the same starting point?

9   *Special Ingredients*

Topic: Diversity

Materials: Chocolate cookie recipe, mixing bowl, ingredients, dough, pre-made cookies

Time: 20-30 minutes   **Space:** Classroom

Activity: You can have your group work together to make cookies, or just have the ingredients along with some cookies you already made. Have each student try the ingredients separately, one at a time, and describe them. Have them tell the function of each ingredient. Then you can have them mix the ingredients and try the cookie dough.

Discussion:

1. Describe what the ingredients tasted like by themselves.
2. What is the role of each individual ingredient?
3. What are our individual roles in the group/class?
4. Why are the ingredients so much better when they are mixed together?
5. What things keep us from mixing together in the group/class/world?
6. What can we do to make sure we mix together more?
7. Each ingredient can represent the different cultures or races in our world. When we all blend together, we can make something special and much more satisfying than if we just stick to ourselves or our own kind of ingredients.
8. How can you relate this activity to people?
9. By ourselves, we are like the individual ingredients. We are not as good separately as we are when we are blended together. Can you give me some examples of things that are better or that could be better if we truly "blended" together? In school/home/work/teams?
10. What are some ingredients we need for success? In school? At home? At work?

10 Everyone Can Contribute

Topic: Diversity, Being unique

Materials: Peas, spaghetti, applesauce, forks, spoons, knives, plates

Time: 20-30 minutes   **Space:** Classroom

Activity: For this activity, you will need to plan a meal or snack for your group to eat. Design the menu so that it would really be difficult eating with only one kind of utensil. The catch is that you will allow everyone only one utensil: a fork, a knife, or a spoon. You can serve a meal of applesauce, peas, and spaghetti. You could give each person only a knife to eat with and watch how he or she may struggle. The discussion during this meal would focus on talents. Everyone has different talents and gifts that are valuable at one time or another. We should use and share our talents and acknowledge that they are valuable. In this simple demonstration, a spoon may not seem too important but sometimes you need a spoon, and only a spoon will do the task.

Discussion:

1. Was it easy to eat these foods using the knife? Why was it difficult?

2. Have you ever tried eating these foods using only a knife?

3. What utensil would you have liked to use?

4. A knife may not have worked as well to eat the applesauce, peas, or spaghetti. What foods do you use a knife for? What foods does a spoon work well for? What foods does a fork work well for?

5. The knife may not have been the best choice for this meal, but it does have its purpose. You may not be able to eat some foods without a knife. Each of the utensils has its own unique purpose that it was designed for. Each of you has your own unique purpose that you were designed for. What are some of the things that make you unique?

6. We all have our own talents and purposes that may not be used all the time. There are times though when only you can do the job because of your unique talents. You may be just the spoon they are looking for! What are some things you know you can do really well that others may not be able to?

11   *We Are Talented Tools*

Topic: Being unique

Materials: Bag full of kitchen/garage tools and gadgets

Time: 20-30 minutes   **Space:** Classroom

Activity: Pass the bag around the group and let the members select a tool from it without looking. Each person then must explain what their tool is and how it is used. You can also have them think of a creative function that the tool could be used for. This could enhance the discussion of their unique talents and purposes.

Discussion:

1. Every tool is unique and was created with one specific purpose in mind, even if it is used in different ways.

2. Every one of you has been created with a unique talent or ability to use.

3. Have the individuals name some of their talents and how they can use them in positive ways.

4. Just like the tools were created for special jobs, what are the ways you can use your special talents?

Relating to Others

12   Words: Uplifters or Weights

Topic: Power of our words

Materials: Balloons, markers, string, helium for balloons

Time: 20-30 minutes   **Space:** Classroom

Activity: This is an activity you can use to initiate a discussion about how the things we say affect others. You will give each person in your group two helium quality balloons. One of the balloons you give them will already be inflated with helium. Have them tie it to a chair or their wrist so it does not float away. Have them blow the other balloon up with their own air and tie it off. Once they have both balloons inflated, they will carefully use a marker to write on the balloons. On the balloon with helium, they should write down a list of words that are positive, encouraging, and uplifting. On the balloon with their own air, they should write down negative, insulting, hurtful words and comments.

After the group is done writing on the balloons, have them share some of the words they have written on each of the balloons. You may want to write down the examples from the balloons. Make a list of positive and negative words/comments. Once the group has shared their words, have them hold each of their balloons above their heads. On your signal, have the group let go of their balloons. You will notice that the balloons with the negative words quickly drop to the ground. The balloons with the positive words will float and stay up. You may want to have the group untie their balloons. It may be a more spectacular effect if you allow the balloons to float to the ceiling, or better yet, into the sky. Now you are ready for the discussion.

Discussion:

1. What happened once you let go of the two balloons?
2. What things were written on the balloons that fell?
3. What was different about the balloon that floated? What words were on it?
4. How can you link this activity to the things we say to people?
5. How do our words affect others?
6. Have you ever been weighted down by something someone else said to you? Can you give some examples of words and comments that might weigh a person down and cause them to "sink?"
7. Have you ever seen another person sink after they heard hurtful words?
8. Can you give some examples of things that people say that might lift you and other people up? Share an example of a comment that lifted you up.
9. Would you rather be a balloon that hits the floor, or one that can reach for the sky?
10. Would you rather carry a bouquet of balloons that floats freely in the air, or one that drags on the ground?
11. How can you make sure that you leave many balloons floating up as high as they can reach everywhere you go?

13 People Shredder

Topic: Power of your words, Gossip/rumors
Materials: Papers that have been shredded, tape, bags
Time: 20-30 minutes   **Space:** Classroom
Activity: You can use this activity to demonstrate the impact that our negative comments and attitudes can have on others. Use this for a group that is not getting along well, has problems with rumors and gossip, or is making fun of certain members. Give each team a bag with a shredded page/picture in it, along with a roll of tape. Use a scissors to cut the piece of paper into strips. You can make the strips big or small, depending on how difficult you want the task to be. Teams must work together to tape the page in its correct order. You can include the real picture if you want so they can have help. You can also use an actual paper shredder to shred the paper. This variation will provide a powerful metaphor of the impact our words can have on others, because it is nearly impossible to put back together.

Discussion:
1. What strategies did they use to tape the sheet back together?
2. What was challenging about the task?
3. How are put downs, insults, and criticisms like the shredded paper?
4. What if we are just kidding? Do our words still hurt others?
5. How do the words we say hurt others?
6. How can we overcome the thought that shredding people is no big deal?
7. Is it just as hard to put shredded people back together?
8. What can you do to make sure people are not being "shredded?"
9. What can we do to "tape" people back together?
10. What are examples of tape?
11. Does the picture that you taped back together look different from before it was ever cut into pieces? What is different about it?
12. Even though the picture is taped back together, it is not quite the same. This can be true for people as well. Some people may not ever fully recover from the tears that other people make in their lives.

14   Clean It Up

Topic: Power of our words, Gossip/rumors

Materials: Cups, paper towels, water

Time: 20-30 minutes   **Space:** Classroom

Activity: Have the group form relay teams of five and line up at one end of the playing area with their teams. Give each person a small cup filled with water, and each team a towel and a pitcher of water. Explain that team members must take turns walking, balancing a cup of water on their foreheads without using their hands, to the other end of the playing area and back. If someone spills the water, he or she must carry the cup back to the team, refill the cup with water, get the towel, carry the cup to the spill, thoroughly wipe up the spill, and start walking balancing the cup from that spot again. Make sure that you emphasize the importance of thoroughly wiping up spills so no one slips. You may need to have extra towels available in case towels get soaked.

Discussion:

1. What was the most difficult aspect of this activity?

2. Would it have been much easier if you did not have to wipe up your spills?

3. Do you think your team would have won if you did not have to wipe up your spills?

4. Do we sometimes hurt others when we get caught up in a competition?

5. When we make mistakes, it can be difficult to clean the mess we make up. (Hurting a person, losing trust, losing a job or relationship, losing money, wrecking a car, etc.)

6. How was cleaning up the spills similar to dealing with the consequences of our actions?

7. What do you think are appropriate ways to deal with the consequences our actions?

8. How can dealing with consequences of actions bring hope, forgiveness, healing?

15   Fragile Feelings

Topic: Our feelings

Materials: Paper napkins, pens or markers, tape

Time: 20-30 minutes   ***Space:*** Classroom

Activity: This activity deals with how delicate our feelings are and how easily we can be hurt. Give each person a napkin. Set out the pens, and have each person draw a picture, word, or symbol that illustrates how he or she is feeling at that time. As kids finish, have them initial their napkins and tape them to a wall. When everyone finishes, have kids form groups of three and take each other on a tour of the feelings that are on the wall. The members of the trios can explain their napkins to each other.

Discussion:

1. Was it difficult to write on the napkin? Why?
2. How can you relate the delicate nature of the napkins to our feelings?
3. Is it easy for our feelings to be hurt?
4. Are some people more fragile than others? Why?
5. Is it easy for our feelings to be helped?
6. Can we always use the same technique to heal/help others? Why not?
7. What can we do to protect our feelings and the feelings of others? In other words, how can we keep our delicate/emotional napkins intact and free from rips?

16   Build Them Up

Topic: Relationships

Materials: Paper, tape measure, a watch

Time: 20-30 minutes   **Space:** Classroom

Activity: This is an activity that can be used to start a discussion on the importance of friends and kindness. Give each group 10 sheets of paper. Tell them that they will have 3 minutes to make the tallest freestanding tower with their ten sheets of paper. The towers must stand for 30 seconds once you call time. Give them one minute to plan and then start their 3-minute building period. You can give them another chance to build a tower. Give them 5-10 more sheets of paper and another 3 minutes.

Discussion:

1. What were some of the difficulties of this activity?
2. Was your group successful in building a tower??
3. What would you change to make this activity easier for you to do?
4. How can you relate building these towers to building relationships with people?
5. If your tower had a strong base/foundation, would it have lasted longer?
6. How can you develop a strong base for your relationships?
7. What things can weaken the base that relationships are built on?
8. What makes it difficult to build relationships with people?
9. How can we make sure that we build long-lasting, strong relationships with people?
10. Were you more successful with your second tower?
11. What things did you learn the first round that helped you to build a better second tower?
12. Sometimes we get a second chance at a friendship or relationship. What are some mistakes we might make that could crumble a relationship?

17 Balloon Joy

Topic: Emotions

Materials: Balloons

Time: 20-30 minutes   **Space:** Classroom

Activity: This short activity will allow your group to think about where joy and happiness come from. Give each person a balloon and ask him or her not to inflate it, but to have fun bouncing it in the air. Let them try to hit it around for a few minutes. The group members will see that hitting an empty balloon is not much fun. Then have the group inflate the balloons and bounce them in the air.

Discussion:

1. Which balloon was more fun: the deflated one or the inflated one?

2. In what ways is the deflated balloon like a person who may be sad or depressed?

3. They are very hard to keep up, no matter what you try.

4. In what ways is the inflated balloon like a person who is happy?

5. They have more energy and bounce around.

6. What kind of person is more fun: a deflated one or a happy one?

7. What are some things that deflate people?

8. What are some things that breathe life and happiness into a person? (You can breathe a breath into a balloon with each example they share.)

9. What can you do for a person who feels depressed and deflated?

18   Friends Rub Off

Topic: Friendship, Peer influence

Materials: Papers with FRIENDS letters on them, pencils, hand wipes

Time: 20-30 minutes   ***Space:*** Classroom

Activity: This is an activity that demonstrates the impact our friends have on us. Before class, print out the word "FRIENDS" in large bubble/block letters about two inches high. During class, give each child a sheet of paper with FRIENDS printed on it and a pencil. Tell them to use the pencil to color in all the letters completely and very dark with the pencil. This may take a few minutes. After they are finished, you will have them rub their fingers over the letters to see that the graphite from the word "FRIENDS" has rubbed off on them. You can also write it on the board and have them come up and wipe part of it off.

Discussion:

1. What happened as you rubbed your fingers over your worksheet?

2. As you wiped your fingers on the word "FRIENDS," some of the chalk, graphite, or ink stayed on your fingers. In what ways do you think your friends can "rub" off on you?

3. Your friends can have a big impact on how you act. What are some of the things that friends can influence? Clothes, music, movies, how we treat others… our choices.

4. We need to choose our friends carefully because we do not want them to influence us in negative ways. Whether you realize it or not, your friends leave an impression on you. It may not be as visible as what you wiped off on your fingertips, but it is there.

5. How can we make sure that we do not let our friends have a negative influence on us? (You can surround yourself with positive people.)

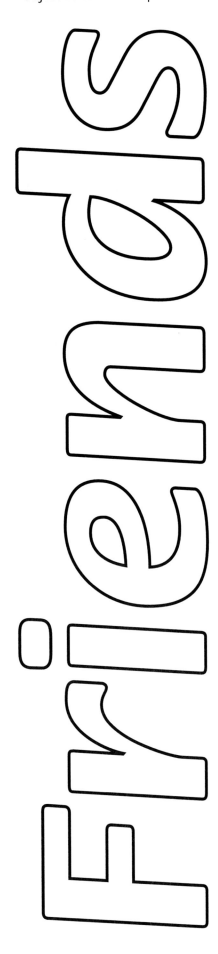

19 Gossip Paper Chain

Topic: Gossip

Materials: Scissors, paper cut into strips, tape or stapler

Time: 20-30 minutes   **Space:** Classroom

Activity: Have the group make a paper chain that is several feet long. Once they have finished, you can relate the paper chain to gossip. You can tape the chain up in your room and have the students add to the chain each time there is a situation with rumors or gossip. That way they will have a reminder all year.

Discussion:

1. Tell the group that once they allow themselves to talk badly about someone, over time it will be difficult to stop saying something bad about everyone they come in contact with. Each person they gossip about will be added to a chain and over time, if they are not careful, the chain will become so long it will be too hard to hold.

2. What can you do to break the chain of gossip?

3. Why do people gossip?

4. What are some *good* things you can gossip about?

20 Clean Slate

Topic: Gossip/rumors, Making mistakes

Materials: Write on boards that erase when you lift the plastic sheet up

Time: 15-30 minutes   **Space:** Classroom

Activity: You can use this activity with gossip or in simply making mistakes since we all do that. For this activity, you will need a few "magic slates." It is a slate with a plastic sheet over the surface. You draw on the slate with a stick. Once you lift the plastic the words disappear. We all probably had one of these as a kid, or at least wish we had. Have your group spend some time writing and drawing on these. They can have as much time as you want to give them, because they can keep wiping the slate clean in order to start over.

Discussion:

1. What happened once you lifted the piece of plastic that covered your drawing?

2. Did any of you lift the plastic sheet after you made a mistake in your drawing or because you wanted to start over?

3. What would be different if we could erase our mistakes just as easily?

4. What would be different if we could just get a fresh, clean start after we made a mistake?

5. Do you think people would make more or fewer mistakes if they knew they could have a fresh start right away?

6. What are some mistakes that we can easily erase?

7. What are some of the mistakes that might not ever be fully erased?

8. What can we do if we are not able to erase our mistakes?

9. Is it still possible to start over once we make a mistake?

10. If you want to use this for gossip, ask them how this might relate to the things we say about other people.

11. We cannot always erase or take back the bad things we say about others. Once we write bad things on other people, they may be there forever.

21 Talk to the Chair

Topic: Gossip/rumors

Materials: Chairs

Time: 15-30 minutes **Space:** Classroom

Activity: Place an empty chair in the middle of the room and then discuss how one good way to avoid gossiping is to imagine the person who you are talking about is sitting in that chair. Ask yourself the following questions as you are picturing the person in the chair: Are you telling the truth? Is the information you are spreading kind or hurtful? Is it necessary for you to pass it on, or are you just doing it because others are? Do you have that person's permission to tell this story or news? Would you say the same things if the person were sitting in the chair in front of you? Here is your final test: if you can't answer yes to all of these questions, then you are probably gossiping and should talk about something else.

Discussion:

1. Why is it so easy to get caught up in gossip?
2. Do you think that your gossip would be controlled or stopped if you tried to think of the person sitting in a chair in front of you?
3. Which of the "chair questions" would cause you to stop gossiping?
4. What is the purpose of gossiping or spreading gossip?
5. Does it hurt people when others gossip about them?
6. What can you do to stop gossip?

22   Toothpaste

Topic: Gossip/rumors

Materials: Small tubes of toothpaste, paper, toothpicks

Time: 20-30 minutes   ***Space:*** Classroom

Activity: You can use a tube of toothpaste to symbolize what comes out of our mouths. You can ask for a volunteer to squeeze some toothpaste out onto his or her finger. The toothpaste symbolizes our words that we speak. You then ask the volunteer to stuff the toothpaste back into the tube. It is an impossible task, no matter how hard you try. You can then talk about how once our words come out, we can never take them back! Another way you can do this is to have each person put a line of toothpaste on a piece of paper. Give each person a toothpick and ask him or her to put the toothpaste back in the tube. They must use the toothpick.

Discussion:

1. What made it difficult to put the toothpaste back in the tube?

2. Once we tell a lie or spread a rumor, what makes it difficult to take those words back?

3. Trying to stuff the toothpaste into the tube can get a little messy. The words we use and lies we spread can also cause a mess in our lives, as well as in other people's lives. Give some examples of problems that can occur after rumors are spread.

4. Just like it is a good idea to control the amount of pressure we use to squeeze the toothpaste out… it is also a good idea to control what we say to and about others so that we do not cause a mess.

23   Clean Words Clean Mouth

Topic: Our bad mouths

Materials: Edible dog poop

Time: 20-30 minutes   **Space:** Classroom

Activity: This can be an unforgettable lesson on the words that come out of our mouths. Our mouth is an important body part, and we certainly would never put dirty things in it. Even though we would never put nasty things in our mouths, we often let nasty things come out of them. Talk about how we would not eat nasty things and yet we speak nasty things. You need to make some edible clay for the lesson so that it looks like dog poop. Make sure that you color it and arrange it so it looks like a pile of dog poop. Once you have your lifelike creation, put it in a plastic baggy. When you are in class, you can pull it out and tell about what your dog left in the backyard. Smell the bag and cringe as though it smells awful.

After discussing the use of bad words, talk about things we would never put in our mouths. Have the class give examples of things you would never put into your mouth. Then ask the group how they would feel if you ate what was in the bag. Make sure that you really live it up during this next part. Take out the pile of poop, smell it and cringe, and then put it in your mouth and eat it. There should be complete silence in the room after you do this and the object lesson should have a lasting impression.

Discussion:

1. Did any of you think I was going to eat the dog poop?
2. What was your reaction when you saw me eat the poop?
3. What is the difference between putting something bad into your mouth and having something bad come out of it?
4. Is it easier to have bad things come out because they hurt others and not us?
5. What can we do to make sure that we do not have nasty things coming out of our mouths?

Here are some recipes I found on the internet you can use for edible dog poop.

Edible Play Dough Recipe

1/3 cup margarine
1/3 cup light corn syrup
1/2 teaspoon salt
1 tablespoon vanilla extract
2 pounds confectioners' sugar
Food coloring

Mix all ingredients together. Make shapes, and then eat.
This dough can be refrigerated in a plastic bag or bowl.

Chocolate Play Clay Recipe

1 (16 ounce) container ready-to-spread chocolate frosting
1 cup creamy peanut butter
1 1/2 cups confectioners' sugar

In a large bowl, combine all the ingredients and mix well. Immediately ready for play! Store in an air-tight container in the refrigerator. It should keep for a couple weeks refrigerated.

Shawn Becker

24 **Damaging Words**

Topic: Negative words/comments.

Materials: Markers, paper plates, shaving cream

Time: 20-30 minutes   **Space:** Classroom

Activity: You will need to take some paper plates and write the words "MEAN" and "BAD" on them. You can do this in front of the students, or have them do it for you. Then cover the plates with shaving cream. Once the plates are covered, ask a student to put the shaving cream back into the can. He or she will tell you that it cannot be done. This will open the door for the discussion. We cannot take back the words we say that hurt people's feelings. You can also have the students write examples of negative words/comments on the plates.

Discussion:

1. What are some examples of hurtful things people your age say to each other?

2. Why do we make hurtful comments?

3. Why were we not able to put the shaving cream back into the can?

4. How can you relate this to not being able to take our words back?

5. What can we do if we have hurt another person with our words?

6. What can we do to make sure we do not hurt each other?

25 Compliment Shower

Topic: Complimenting others

Materials: Ping-pong balls, marker, bucket or net, string

Time: 20-30 minutes **Space:** Classroom

Activity: For this activity, you will need a large quantity of ping-pong balls. You will need to have about 3-4 per person. Before the activity, you will use a marker to write positive compliments on the ping-pong balls. You can write one on each ball. Make sure that the comments are personal or personality characteristics. Here are some examples: awesome athlete, sweet smile, friendly, likes to laugh, leader, good ideas, easy-going, and so on. Once you get all the balls filled out, your entire group is going to experience a compliment shower. You will need to suspend the balls in a net or basket from a hook or light fixture in the room. You can also stand on chairs holding the net.

When you are ready for the activity, you will ask the group to sit close together on the floor under the balls. Explain that they'll soon be "showered with compliments," which they're supposed to share with their peers. You can then dump the balls on kids' heads. The kids will then each grab a ball, read what it says, and find someone to give that compliment to. Make sure no one receives more than 3-4 ping-pong balls. You can have kids take home their ping-pong balls as reminders of how awesome they are.

Discussion:

1. How did it feel to receive the "compliment" balls?
2. Was it difficult to find people to give a ball to?
3. Why is hard for some of us to receive compliments?
4. Why is hard for some of us to give compliments?
5. What would be different if everyone was showered with compliments every day?
6. What can we do as a group or class to make this happen?
7. If compliments are free, why are so few given away?
8. Make a list of people you are going to make an effort to compliment.

Working With Others

26   You Can't Comb Your Hair

Topic: Helping others

Materials: Combs or hairbrushes

Time: 20-30 minutes   **Space:** Classroom or larger space

Activity: This is an activity that easily leads into a discussion of how we cannot do everything ourselves. Bring a few combs or brushes to the class, or have them use their own. Have students comb their hair, with the stipulation that they cannot bend their elbows. This is quite a funny sight to see them trying to comb their hair with straight arms. They will find that the task is basically impossible. Have the group members partner up with another person. One member in the pair will use the comb and try combing their partner's hair again with only straight arms. This time it is possible, because you are able to help each other out. There are things we cannot do for ourselves, and another person must do it for us.

Discussion:

1. What are some other things that we cannot do by ourselves?

2. Was it difficult to have another person comb your hair? Is it difficult to have others help you?

3. Have any of you ever been in a situation where other people had to help you with things you normally did yourself? (Broken arm, broken foot, etc.)

4. How do you feel when you have to ask others to help you?

5. Is there anything wrong with asking another person to help you?

6. Why is it difficult for some people to ask for help?

7. What are some things you are working on that can be finished if you ask for help?

8. Who are some people who have helped you and or that could help you?

27   Wall Lean

Topic: Helping others
Materials: Dollar bills, paper wads
Time: 20-30 minutes   **Space:** Classroom
Activity: This is a task that seems impossible to complete and is a good way to challenge your group. It can be used to demonstrate that things that seem to be impossible are possible when you work together with others. They should not be standing by anything they can hold onto. They will lean against the wall, placing their shoulder and inside foot flat against the wall. If they are standing with their right shoulder against the wall, their right foot must stay tight against the wall. The side of their foot will be tight to the wall. The challenge is that they must lift their outside leg without moving their shoulder or inside foot from the wall. If they have their right shoulder and foot against the wall, they must lift their left foot off of the ground. They will try to cheat, so you have to make sure that they keep their shoulder tight to the wall. If you need to, you can place a piece of paper between their shoulder and the wall. The paper cannot slip out.

You can add some fun and motivation by placing a paper ball on the foot they have to lift. I usually use a dollar bill and tell them they can keep it if they are able to lift their foot. If they follow your rules, they will not be able to lift their foot. Try it yourself so you know what it feels like. I usually let them try it a few times, giving them a hard time because it is only a piece of paper. You can draw it out a few times if you want to before you make your point. What you can do then is tell them that you can do it. Have them gather around as you make the impossible… possible. Stand like you asked them to do. Have someone come and stand next to you. Then place your hand on the person's shoulder and lift your outside leg. You cannot do it without another person's help, which is the point of the lesson. Now you can launch into a discussion about how we can achieve much more when we work together. Try to make as many links as you can to the things their group can accomplish by working together.

Discussion:
1. Did you think you would be able to accomplish this task?
2. Did you think it could be easily done?
3. What made it difficult/impossible to do?
4. What are some other things that we cannot do by ourselves?
5. Is it difficult to have others help you?
6. Is there anything wrong with asking another person to help you?
7. What are some reasons why people do not ask for help?
8. What are some things you are working on that can be finished if you ask for help?
9. Who are some people who have helped you and or that could help you?

28 Concentrated Effort

Topic: Working together

Materials: Magnifying glass, piece of regular glass, paper, sunny day

Time: 20-30 minutes   **Space:** Classroom or larger space

Activity: Take your group outside and give one person the magnifying glass and another person the normal glass. Your challenge is to see who can burn a hole in the paper the fastest. Give enough time for several people to try it. You will find that it is only possible with the magnifying glass. There are many mini-lessons built into this one. They all deal in some way with focus, concentrating your efforts, and working together. Here are some examples: In order to get quickly to the heart of a problem with a solution, you have to have concentrated effort; magnifying your focus and efforts means giving real concentration and the result is magnified power; look what unusual powers glass can have when it is concentrated in that one spot; what can happen when a group works together to solve a problem? If a group is working as a team focusing on their goal, they can achieve it more quickly because of their increased power.

Discussion:

1. Which method was able to burn the paper: the magnifying glass or the regular glass? Why?
2. What is the difference between the regular glass and the magnifying glass?
3. What does it mean when something is magnified?
4. What difference does it make when you focus and concentrate your efforts?
5. Do you believe that your class/group can achieve more if you are all working together?
6. What do you need to change in order to magnify your power in this group?
7. What do you think you could accomplish if you magnified your power by concentrating and focusing?

29 Ripple Effect

Topic: Serving others, Random acts of kindness

Materials: Container with water and a rock

Time: 20-30 minutes   **Space:** Classroom or larger space

Activity: We have all watched water ripples spread out in a puddle, lake, or pond. We are going to recreate that same visual example in this activity. Ask the group to watch what happens when you drop a rock into a still pond or pan of water. Have the group describe what happens after you drop the rock into the water. You will notice a single ring forms first around the rock and it will then radiate outwards into more and more rings. The ring starts in the center and keeps spreading to the outside. This is what happens with a good deed. The good feeling that both people have, those who do the good deed, and those who receive, radiates outward and affects more and more people around them.

Discussion:

1. Why do the water rings keep spreading outward?

2. Have you ever been the victim of a good deed?

3. What does it feel like when people do good things for you or say nice things to you?

4. Just like how the water rings formed from one rock or one action, a good deed can spread into an ever-expanding ring of positive influence and action. When good deeds bump into each other, they form another good deed, just like the water ripples.

30 Popping Power

Topic: Working together, Sharing our resources

Materials: Popcorn seeds, small cups, bowl, popcorn popper

Time: 20-30 minutes   **Space:** Classroom

Activity: You will either have to have a popcorn popper to use or pop some up ahead of time. If you have it made ahead of time, keep it out of sight until the end of the activity when you make your point. You will give each student a cup with a few popcorn seeds in it. Once everyone has a cup, tell them that they can keep theirs, or they can give it back. You will take your cup and pour your seeds in a bowl. Ask again if anyone wants to add their seeds to yours and give them back. (Some might want to keep theirs for themselves, but that's okay.) After students add their seeds to the bowl with yours, you can say, "Look! I had just a little bit, and you had just a little bit, but when we put all of ours together, look how much we have!" You can then get out the popper and add the seeds to it. Pop up the batch and compare the volume of the unpopped seeds to the popped popcorn.

Discussion:

1. Was it difficult for you to share your seeds and give them back?

2. What made you want to add your seeds to the bowl with mine?

3. When the popcorn was popped, how did it compare to the bowl of unpopped seeds?

4. When you shared and gave me your seeds, we ended up with a lot more popcorn than any of us could have had by ourselves.

5. When we freely give from our heart, we can get much more back. When we work together as a team, we can get much more accomplished.

6. What are some of things that people your age can give? (Time, money, ideas, kindness, helping out, etc.)

7. Make the point that if we do not give, we get to keep what we have or had originally. When we are unwilling to share or give, we miss out on the opportunity of a larger return.

8. What would you rather have right now: the unpopped seeds or the hot popcorn?

31   Lean on Me

Topic: Helping others, Leaning on others

Materials: Pillows or cushions or do it outside in the grass/snow

Time: 20-30 minutes   **Space:** Classroom

Activity: Have everyone stand an arm's length apart, with a pillow behind each person. Tell kids to place their feet together and their hands at their sides. Say, *"The object of this activity is to sit gently on the ground without crashing. You may not move your feet or use your hands. Ready? Go."* Most group members will probably fall on the way to the floor or at least have a little "thud" at the end. You can briefly talk about whether it was easy or difficult to accomplish the task. Tell the group that you are going to have them attempt it again with a partner. Have them pair up and stand back to back as they attempt to sit down. Having a partner should make sitting down much easier. You will have the pairs do it a third time by having the partners stand back to back with their arms locked together. They can attempt to sit down once their arms are locked.

Discussion:

1. Why was it difficult to sit without falling the first time?

2. How did you improve during the second and third attempts?

3. What are ways we fall in everyday life?

4. How is the way your partner kept you from falling like or unlike the way people in your life can keep you from falling? (Teachers, parents, friends, counselors, etc.)

5. Working with others can make things easier for us to accomplish.

6. How can we lean on others when we feel like we're about to fall in life?

7. Who do you have in your life that keeps you from falling or catches you when you fall?

8. Is there anyone you need or would like in your life to help you when you fall?

32   Two Halves Working Together

Topic: Working together

Materials: Clothespins, paper, napkins, pencils

Time: 20-30 minutes   **Space:**   Classroom or larger space

Activity: You will need to take the clothespins apart so that you have two halves. Give a half to each student. Have pairs work together to hold an object by using their non-dominant hand to hold one half of the clothespin. Allow them to try holding a variety of objects with the separated clothespins. Then give each person a clothespin that is put together. Have them pick up the objects now and compare their success. Ask them which way was easier to hold the objects.

Discussion:

1. What made it difficult to hold the objects when the clothespin was in two pieces?

2. The clothespins that are connected together work much more effectively and efficiently. What are some ways that we can work together in this group/ class?

3. What difference would it make if we were all working together?

4. What keeps people your age from working together?

33 *Strength in Strands*

Topic: Helping others, Working together

Materials: Dry and cooked spaghetti

Time: 20-30 minutes   **Space:** Classroom

Activity: This is a lesson to demonstrate that there is strength in numbers when you stick or work together. You can first show that by yourself, your power is limited. Demonstrate this by holding a piece of dry spaghetti straight up and down on a table. Push down on top of the single strand until it breaks. You can keep adding more and more strands to show that the more people you have working with you, the stronger you are. You can also take the whole bundle of dry spaghetti and push down on it. The bundle will be able to stand up to much more stress. As you push down with more force, you may find that some of the outer strands break, but most of them will not.

You can also use the spaghetti for a lesson on positive and negative influences. You will need to make some spaghetti and let it dry for a while. Before the class, wrap some dry spaghetti around the wet stuff and hold it together with tape or a rubber band. Hold this bundle straight up and down on the table and test it. When you push down on the bundle, your group will see that it cannot withstand much pressure, even though it has dry strands around it. This is because the wet spaghetti was rubbed off and weakened the dry strands. This can be a good visual lesson to use when you are talking about choosing peers and friends to hang around with. They may be compromising us, even if we do not realize it.

Discussion:

1. How much pressure did it take to break the single strand?
2. Can people stand up against a lot of pressure, or would it be better to have a group around you?
3. What are some things that might put a lot of pressure and stress on people your age?
4. What are your options when you start to feel like there is a lot of weight or pressure being forced down on you?
5. In what ways does the bundle of dry spaghetti relate to teamwork?
6. How much pressure can the wet spaghetti withstand?
7. How was the wet spaghetti like a negative friend, peer, or role model?
8. Tell me how hanging around negative people can affect you, just like the wet spaghetti weakened the dry strands.
9. Are we always able to recognize who is having a negative influence on us?
10. Are we always willing to admit that some of our friends might not be positive people for us to hang around?
11. Why are we not always willing to see this?
12. What will you take from this activity and apply to your everyday life?

34 Leaders Stand Out

Topic: Leadership

Materials: Penny, dime, nickel, Susan B. Anthony dollar coin, blindfolds

Time: 20-30 minutes   **Space:** Classroom

Activity: This is an activity you can use to demonstrate the importance of standing out. Some of us stand out as positive leaders, while many of us just blend together, so it is hard to tell who we are or what we stand for. You will ask for some volunteers to stand in front of the group. Have the volunteers close their eyes or use a blindfold. Give them one coin at a time and see if they can guess what it is. After each guess, tell them how many they got right. They should be able to correctly guess all of them, except for the Susan B. Anthony dollar. It feels a lot like a quarter, so they will assume it is one. The Susan B. Anthony dollar had to be taken out of circulation because it was not different enough. It did not stand out like the rest of the coins do.

Discussion:

1. Which was the easiest coin for you to identify?
2. Which was most difficult? Why?
3. How can a person your age stand out in positive ways?
4. How can a person your age stand out in negative ways?
5. Why is it hard for people your age to stand out as leaders in positive ways?
6. What are some ways that leaders stand out?
7. What things here in school can help you stand out as a leader?
8. What can you do in this group/classroom to stand out as a leader?
9. Make sure that you are different and that you stand out from the negative people.
10. Are people going to know what you stand for, or do you blend together with everyone else?

Goals

35   Chasing Elusive Bubbles

Topic: Goal Setting, Focusing on the right things

Materials: Small container of bubbles for everyone

Time: 20-30 minutes   **Space:** Classroom

Activity: This is an activity that demonstrates the importance of what we are striving for. Hand out the bubbles to the members in your group. Once everyone has a bottle, tell him or her that they can open them up and begin blowing bubbles. You can allow them to do this for a few minutes. It can be interesting to watch how much they enjoy it.

After a few minutes, ask them to stop and put the bubbles away, or have one person blow them while everyone else watches.

Discussion:

1. What do you think of as you watch the bubbles float?

2. Why do people, especially kids, enjoy bubbles so much?

3. What characteristics of bubbles draw us in?

4. Why do kids chase bubbles?

5. What happens as they try to catch them? They pop!

6. No matter how many pop, they keep trying to catch one.

7. What are some of the bright, flashy, sparkling, mesmerizing things that people your age chase? What are the bubbles we are going after? (i.e., popularity, fame, money, relationships, grades, power, etc.)

8. Just like the bubbles, these things won't last as we try to catch them. Sometimes they may stay just out of our reach no matter how hard we try.

9. What are the things that people your age should spend time chasing?

10. What are the bubbles that will last?

36 Caught in a Web

Topic: How our problems can affect us if we do not let them go.

Materials: Ball of string

Time: 20-30 minutes   **Space:** Classroom

Activity: This one can demonstrate how our problems can trap us. You ask your group to stand in a circle. The first person takes the ball of string and wraps some around his or her finger. He or she then shares with the group something that has been a problem. The individual then throws the ball of string to someone else in the circle. The next person does the same and so on until all the group members are holding the string. They will all be connected in a web.

Once everyone is connected to the web, you can have one person slowly and gently move their "web" hand. Have the group observe what happens when just one person moves. (The entire group is impacted.) This can demonstrate how one of our problems can take over and impact every area of our lives if we don't deal with it effectively.

Discussion:

1. We are all in danger of getting caught in webs. What are some things that might trap people your age?

2. What are some webs you can get caught in?

3. What can we do to remain "web free?" It could be a thought pattern, a feeling, a group of friends, a dream, and so forth that traps us.

37 Trapped with Your Problems

Topic: How our problems can affect us if we do not let them go

Materials: A jar with a narrow opening and a ball/object

Time: 20-30 minutes   **Space:** Classroom

Activity: This is an activity that can be used to show how holding onto our problems really holds us back from what we can accomplish. You need to have this activity ready before this lesson. You have to get a jar with a narrow opening. Make sure that your hand can fit in the opening. You want to put a ball in the jar but make sure that it is just a little smaller than the opening. You are going to have a person put their hand in the jar and grab the ball. The catch is that if the opening is the right size, they will not be able to pull their hand out while holding the ball. The metaphor is that if they hold on to their problems, they can get stuck.

Discussion:

1. Why was it difficult/impossible to remove your hand while holding on to the ball?

2. What are some things we hold on to that trap us that could be represented by the ball?

3. Why is it difficult to let go of the things that trap us?

4. Do we always know that we are being trapped?

5. What do people need to do so that they can be freed from their personal traps?

6. What things are you being trapped by because you are unwilling to drop them?

7. What do you need to do to free yourself?

38 *Melting Your Bitterness*

Topic: Holding grudges

Materials: Ice cubes

Time: 20-30 minutes   **Space:** Classroom

Activity: Give each student an ice cube. Have each of them hold the ice cube over their heads and race to see who can melt their "grudge" the fastest, using only their hands. Explain that a grudge can leave you cold, just like this piece of ice.

Discussion:

1. How difficult was it for you to melt your ice cube?

2. Were any of you in pain toward the end?

3. A grudge can leave you feeling bitter cold, just like the ice cube did.

4. It can also leave behind tears that stream down your face, just like the water that was dripping on your head from the ice.

5. Some people say that a grudge can leave you cold. What does this mean?

6. Just like trying to melt the ice cube, it can be difficult to get rid of a grudge. What do you think it takes to make a grudge melt? (Risk-taking, forgiveness, apologies, the truth, letting go, etc.)

7. Letting go can help you melt the grudges quickly, like using a hair dryer to melt the ice cubes.

8. What are some grudges people your age may hold?

9. How can letting go of a grudge help people?

39   Taking Action

Topic: Making an effort in your life, Setting goals

Materials: Balloons

Time: 20-30 minutes   **Space:** Classroom

Activity: You will need to have two deflated balloons in each of your two pockets. You can tell the group you have something in your pockets and ask them to guess. After a few guesses, pull out one of the balloons. You can say that balloons are usually a lot of fun to hit around and play with. Explain to them that there must be something wrong with yours because it is not that much fun. You can try hitting it around as you are talking and they will be able to see that it is not much fun. Ask the group if they know why it is not much fun. Obviously, because you haven't blown it up. Respond with surprise... "You mean I have to put something into it?" "I have to make an effort?" Then blow it up... let it go... blow it up again and tie it.

Explain to the group that the balloon that is full of air cannot be hidden easily. Pull out the other balloon from your pocket. Point out that no one knew it was there, since they could not see it. This balloon has a lot of potential, just like all of you. All it needs is goals and energy put into it.

Discussion:

1. Your life can be like the balloon. You have to put time and effort into your life in order to make it a good one. What are some things that you have to put into your life to make it full like the balloon? (i.e., goals, education, relationships, skills, values)

2. Would you believe that some people try and hide their talents and potential? Why might someone do this?

3. You do not want a life like the deflated balloon. You should want a life that you put action into. This kind of life cannot be hidden, just like the balloon that is all filled up. You should set your goals so that everyone can see them. That way, you will be living a life that makes you happy and influences others.

4. Our goals can be like the deflated balloon. We need to put time, energy, and effort into our goals in order for them to be accomplished.

5. What are some goals that people your age might have?

6. What is necessary to accomplish those goals?

40 Stretching Limits

Topic: Setting goals, Taking risks, Pushing yourself

Materials: Packing wrap like the kind sold at a hardware store

Time: 30-50 minutes   **Space:** Classroom

Activity: Have 8-10 students stand in a tight circle so that they are huddled close together. You will then wrap them a few times, at their waist level, with the packing wrap. (I found some at Menards that is 6-8 inches wide that works well because it stretches the best). I wrap them three times, being careful to keep it in the same place on them so that it is 3 layers think. Then you place 4 objects 4-5 feet away from them, making a square around them. What they have to do is move over and pick the objects up without breaking the wrap or stepping outside of it. The group will usually do this by shuffling to the objects and bending down to pick them up.

After they retrieve the 4 objects, have them go back to where they started and then place the objects back where they originally were. This time tell the group that they have to get the objects without shuffling around. They also cannot move from the center of where they are standing. What this means is that the entire group cannot walk around like they did the first time. They have to figure out that the wrap will stretch and that they must stretch it, staying within it, in order to reach the objects. Once they get the four objects, have them go back to their original spot again. Place the four objects in their original spots as well. Then have the group slowly move back as they stretch the wrap. Have them keep moving outward, stretching the wrap until it breaks. If it is done correctly, they will find that they are standing right next to the objects, or even beyond them.

You can have them make observations about where they are standing in relation to where the objects are. The objects should be located within their wrap circle that they stretched out. It can be a rich discussion as you talk about why they did not stretch the wrap to begin with.

Discussion:

1. Explain why you did not stretch the wrap the first time?
2. What did you allow to limit yourself during this activity?
3. Was it too big of a risk to stretch the wrap right away?
4. Why did you later feel comfortable stretching the wrap?
5. What are some things that limit you or people your age from taking risks?
6. Give examples from your life when you were afraid to take risks.
7. Have you ever been rewarded for taking risks? Explain how.
8. What are some areas you need or would like to take more risks in?
9. What goals could you reach if you allowed yourself to really "stretch?"

Personal Character

41 Insight into Integrity

Topic: Integrity, Honesty

Materials: You need a soft throw able object for this activity

Time: 20-30 minutes   **Space:** Classroom

Activity: This activity deals with "Integrity" and is about honor, making decisions about one's actions, and honesty. It can help your group understand and discuss what *Integrity* is/means. *Integrity,* simply defined, is who you are when no one else is around. Who are you and what choices do you make when there is nobody around to see or catch you? Do you do the "right" thing when no one will ever know the difference? The group stands in a circle and throws an object from person to person around and across the circle, following these rules.

1. Everyone must remain silent once the activity starts.

2. You can only move to throw or catch the object.

3. You must make a good throw or catch.

   Any time a rule is violated, you must back out of the circle while the rest of the people keep going. Do the activity 2-3 times to give people another chance to increase and renew their Integrity. You may want to do this in two smaller groups and start over once you are down to just a few people left.

   There is another rule you can add after a few practice rounds.

4. If the ball is not thrown to you but you move, flinch, or try to catch it, you have to take yourself out of the game. There will be a lot more people eliminated with this rule. We have a hard time not moving if it is thrown in our direction.

Discussion:

1. What does *Integrity* mean?

2. What are the characteristics a person with *Integrity* has?

3. Is it easy to always do the "right" thing?

4. What are some reasons people your age find it difficult to "do the right thing?" (Peer pressure, lack of strong values/morals, sense of right vs. wrong)

5. What things make it difficult for people your age to maintain their *Integrity?*

6. Who are you when no one else is around?

7. Is it possible to lose your *Integrity?*

8. Do you get another chance to gain your *Integrity* back if you lose it? It may not be as easy as in the activity, but you can always choose a fresh start.

9. What would it mean to you if other people said that you were a person bursting with *Integrity?*

10. What changes can you make as an individual to increase your *Integrity* and keep it at a high level?

11. Who will be first to notice that you have changed and gained *Integrity?*

Shawn Becker

42   Nowhere to Hide

Topic: Guilt, Integrity

Materials: Tall glass containers, cola soda, buttons, spoon

Time: 15 to 30 minutes.   **Space:** Classroom or outside area

Activity: This activity deals with the compulsion we all have to keep our lies hidden from others. How well can you keep a secret? Have you ever felt that after doing something wrong, if you just keep it a secret no one will ever find out? Most of us have felt that way, but did you know that no matter how hard we try to keep our lies a secret, they have a way of becoming known? Let me show you what I mean. Pour some of the soda into the glass (about 4 ounces). Explain that the glass represents you, and the soda represents a place where we hide our bad secrets, maybe deep inside our heart where we do not want anybody to know. Show the group the buttons and explain that they represent the lies that we tell and other bad things we want to hide. Give some examples of what the buttons might represent: a lie you told a friend, something you stole, cheating on a test, using the phone when your parents asked you not to. Explain that you are going to drop all the buttons into the soda where they will be hidden from our sight. Drop the buttons in and see what happens. In a few seconds, the buttons will float to the top.

Ask the group if they can see the buttons. They appear to be hidden, but will eventually appear by floating to the surface. We can only keep our lies and bad stuff hidden for a little while; eventually, lies have a way of coming to the surface. We cannot keep them hidden forever. Instead of trying to hide this bad stuff, we need to do what is right. Even though we have been trying to keep this bad stuff hidden in our hearts and lives, we can get rid of it. We can be clean again. You can take the buttons out with the spoon and say that now our heart/life is clean again.

Discussion:

1. What are some things that people your age try to cover up?
2. What makes it difficult to keep them covered up?
3. What role does our conscience play in covering up the bad stuff?
4. What rises to the top in your life?
5. Can we ever truly cover something up and keep it hidden?
6. What role does guilt play when we are hiding things?
7. Why is it so hard to tell the truth at times?
8. What do you need to do to make sure that your heart is clean?

43   The Power Within

Topic: Personal power.

Materials: Bottle of club soda, dish tub, or plastic container.

Time: 20-30 minutes   **Space:** Classroom

Activity: This is a good activity to demonstrate the power we have stored up inside of us. We all have it there and just need the right thing to release it. Grab the bottle of soda and say, "A fun thing to do with carbonated drinks is to shake them up and watch them fizz!" I have a bottle of carbonated water right here. You should use carbonated water because it won't get sticky like other sodas if people get some on them. Tell the group that there is a lot of power resting in a bottle of soda like this. If you just let it sit and do nothing to it, it's not very exciting, nothing happens. However, if I were to shake it up . . . Hold your thumb over the opening and shake the soda while you talk.

You may choose to allow some water to spray on your group. This will create a lot of excitement, and the kids love it! If this is not appropriate for your group, then have a container to catch the water as it foams over the top of the bottle. Tell the group that there is so much power being released that you can't hold it anymore! Look at all that activity and action! That's exciting! Something's happening, where before it was just boring.

Discussion:
1. Did you know that there was that much power inside this bottle of water?
2. What made it possible for all that energy to come from the bottle of water?
3. Have you ever thought about the power and energy you have stored up inside of you? Each of you is like this bottle of water. You have a lot of energy inside and you just need the right thing to shake you up so you can release it.
4. What are some ways that people release their personal power? Setting goals, helping others, sports, hobbies, jobs, making others laugh, writing, and singing are some examples.
5. Some people release their personal power in negative ways, such as anger, bullying, and fighting.
6. What are some things that shake you up and get you excited about releasing your personal power?
7. What are some goals you have?

Shawn Becker

44 Control over Your Circumstances

Topic: Resiliency.

Materials: Candle, matches, at least two round balloons, water

Time: 20-30 minutes   **Space:** Classroom

Activity: We all have problems we deal with in our lives. For this exciting illustration, you will need a candle and two good quality round balloons. You will need to fill one balloon with water and leave the other deflated until you give the message. When you are ready to begin, ask the group the following, "What if I put a water balloon into the flame of the candle?" This should get their get attention, because they know what will happen. Ask them if they think you can do it without breaking the balloon. Explain to them that there is a scientific principle that will allow you to put the water balloon into the flame without it bursting. The water spreads the heat so that the balloon will not pop. Light the candle and then blow up the deflated balloon. Keep the water balloon hidden until you need it.

There are things that come into a person's life that are stressful, depressing, and very painful. There are circumstances and situations that, like this flame, can hurt and even destroy us. Take for instance this balloon. Let's say it represents a person's life. If we bring this balloon into the fire, it is destroyed. Carefully touch the balloon to the flame, and it will pop. This will get everyone's attention. Continue by saying that many people, when their lives come into contact with fiery trials and hardships, can often be destroyed "under the circumstances." They might just give up or suffer helplessly. Now you can grab the balloon that has water in it. You may want to give examples of things that people in your group or class struggle with, as you get ready to use the water-filled balloon. You will hold the balloon by the stem over the flame. Carefully touch it to the flame, or hold it directly above for 10 seconds. It should not pop as you pass it over the flame. The group should be amazed by your "magic" trick. Practice this at home so that you are sure it will work.

Discussion:

1. Did you believe me when I told you that I could touch a balloon to the flame without popping it? Why or Why Not?

2. Do you believe me that each one of you can stand up to every fire that touches you without popping?

3. What are some things people have inside or around them that can protect them and help dissipate the heat they are experiencing? Family, friends, faith, or personality?

4. What are some situations that act as a fire trying to burn us in our lives?

5. What are some other things you can do to put out the "fires" in your life?

6. What was the difference between the first and second balloon? It had something inside of it that helped protect it.

7. Some people are like the first balloon. They blow up and fall apart as soon as life gets difficult for them. Some people are like the second balloon. They can resist all kinds of stress, pressure, and heat. What is the difference between these two types of people?

45 Presentation Is Everything

Topic: Our words and actions reflect who we are inside

Materials: Nicely decorated cake, plates, forks

Time: 20-30 minutes   **Space:** Classroom

Activity: You can use this at the end of a discussion on character and positive choices. You will bring a beautifully decorated cake into class. Ask the students if they would like a piece of the cake. Choose someone that said yes and **with your hand,** grab out a piece of cake, slap it down on a plate, and hand it to them. The individual will be a little surprised and possibly disgusted. You will then slice a nice piece of cake to show the contrast. Now you can let the class members have a piece of cake, asking how they would like their piece served. You can use this activity to show that people can be more or less attractive and appealing, depending on how they "serve" themselves.

How we present ourselves to others is very important in whether they will want to be our friends or not. It matters how we dress and what we say and how honest we are because we are "serving and presenting" ourselves at all times, even when we don't think about it. If presentation is everything, make sure that you are presenting the person you want others to see. You want to be like the nicely cut piece of cake, not the one that was slapped down on the plate with my hand.

Discussion:

1. What were your reactions once you saw me slap the cake down with my hands?

2. How many of you did not want a piece of cake if I used my hands to serve it?

3. What is wrong with using my hands to serve a beautiful cake?

4. What was different about the pieces that I cut with a knife and served with a spatula? The piece of cake I cut and served still looked nice.

5. Your decision to have a piece of cake depended on how I presented it to you. The same is true for each of us. How we present ourselves to others affects how they decide to treat us and whether or not they will accept us.

6. How do the people you trust "present" themselves to you? (Trustworthy, nice, funny, etc.)

7. How do you want to present yourself to others?

8. Are you being seen by others like you want to? What things would you like to change about your presentation?

46 Good Stuff Rises to the Top

Topic: Good habits, Perseverance

Materials: Popcorn, ping-pong ball, jar

Time: 20-30 minutes   **Space:** Classroom or larger space

Activity: Here is a fun object lesson. You will need to fill a large clear jar (larger than a quart, if possible) half way up with popped popcorn. You will then take a ping-pong ball and push it to the bottom of the popcorn. Then put the lid on and swirl the jar around. While doing this for a few seconds, the ping-pong ball will rise to the top of the popcorn. After you show this demonstration and let everyone else do it, then discuss what habits and traits a person needs to develop that would help them rise above the negative situations in their lives.

Discussion:

1. How many of you thought that the ping-pong ball would actually rise to the top?

2. Is it possible to hide our bad habits forever? Is it possible to keep our good habits or talents hidden forever?

3. Why do people try to hide their bad habits?

4. In this activity, the ball can also represent you and your life. The popcorn can be the negative people, forces, or circumstances that you have to overcome. What are some of things that try to hold people down?

5. Do people ever rise to the top or pull themselves out from under negative forces?

6. What are some examples of people who did not let "life" keep them down?

7. What makes it possible for a person to rise up? What are the traits or characteristics that a person has who rises to the top?

8. What role does perseverance play in rising to the top?

47   Magnetic Attraction

Topic: Our reputation

Materials: Metal shavings, magnet

Time: 20-30 minutes   **Space:** Classroom or larger space

Activity: This activity can demonstrate that the people we hang around with can define our reputation. You will need to spread the metal shavings on the top of your table. You will then pass the magnet over the top of the table. If you take a magnet and pass it over the top of some metal shavings, they will jump up and cling to the magnet. The magnet does not have to physically touch the shavings, just come close. We should always make sure that we hang out with people of positive character because our reputation is like those metal shavings. If you are around rebellious, negative, shady people, their reputation will eventually stick to you. Even if you never actually do anything bad yourself, by hanging around dishonest or evil friends, that is the reputation you draw to yourself like a magnet.

Discussion:

1. Why were the metal shavings drawn toward the magnet?
2. Did the magnet always have to touch the metal in order to still pull it? How was it able to attract the metal from a distance?
3. The magnet has power that allows it to pull the metal. Do you think that people have power to pull others into their group?
4. How is the power of the magnet like the power of certain people and groups?
5. Why do the people who are troublemakers try to pull others in?
6. What are the payoffs from having a bad reputation?
7. What can you do to make sure you are able to resist the pull?
8. What groups are you attracted to? Why do they interest you?
9. Who can tell me what a reputation is?
10. What are some reputations people your age might have?
11. What are some positive reputations? Negative?
12. Is it important to have a good reputation? Why?
13. Do you know anyone who has a bad reputation?
14. What causes their bad reputation?
15. Do you know any "good" people who have a bad reputation just because they hang with a particular group?
16. What does it mean to be guilty by association?
17. What can you do to make sure that you are attractive to and attracted by people with good reputations?

48 *Character Armor*

Topic: Having a thick skin, Perseverance

Materials: Oranges, water, clear container

Time: 20-30 minutes   ***Space:*** Classroom or larger space

Activity: You will need two oranges and two clear containers filled with water for this activity. You will need to put the oranges in the clear container to show that they both float. Have class members come up with things that both strengthen or represent personal armor people wear, and things that weaken or distress the armor. Each time you discuss something that weakens the armor, peel a slice off from one of the oranges. Keep going until the whole orange is peeled. You will peel only one of the oranges. Float the two oranges a few times during the lesson to see how they are doing. When the whole orange is peeled, the orange without the armor (peel) sinks to the bottom.

Discussion:

1. What are some examples of armor that people use to protect themselves physically, mentally, spiritually, and emotionally? (Talk things out, relax, exercise, pray, rest, remain optimistic, etc.)

2. Just like with the orange, we can have pieces of our personal protection/armor peeled away over time. What are some things that would peel off our armor?

3. What can we do to make sure that our armor stays strong?

4. Is it possible to repair our armor if it does become damaged? Give some examples of positive things we can do to make our armor strong again.

49   Personal Protection

Topic: Dealing with difficult things in our lives

Materials: Protective pads, helmets, goggles, glasses, gloves, boots, umbrella

Time: 20-30 minutes   **Space:** Classroom or larger space

Activity: You will need to put together a variety of items that we use to protect our-selves. You can use the items listed above or find an assortment of your own. Be creative because there are many things/materials we use. You can have the group try the items on as you discuss the protective function.

Discussion:

1. Why do we wear these things?

2. What things on our bodies did these items protect?

3. Why is it important to protect our bodies from harm?

4. Can we protect ourselves from being hurt all the time?

5. What are some things that hurt us?

6. Can we protect ourselves from these things?

7. What can we use as "personal protection" when we encounter the situa-tions/things you listed above?

8. If we put on a bike helmet, does it mean we will never fall off our bikes? If we put on gloves in the winter when we go outside, does it mean the tempera-ture will be warmer outside?

9. Just because we use these things to protect our bodies does not mean that we still won't fall, get rained on, or be stuck in a snowstorm again. So wear-ing and using these things won't stop the "accidents" or tough times from happening, but the protection will give us new ways to deal with them.

10. There is no way to totally protect ourselves from the trials and accidents in life, but we can make sure that we are protected and have ways to deal with life.

11. What are some things you can do to arm yourself so that you will be pre-pared for what life throws at you?

50 Absorption

Topic: Keeping an open mind

Materials: Sponge, rock, bowl, water, squirt gun

Time: 15 to 30 minutes.   **Space:** Classroom or outside area

Activity: If you want to add more impact to the lesson, you can cut the sponge into the shape of a heart. You will begin the lesson by first placing the rock in the bowl. Ask the students to tell you some properties of a rock. Tell them it is a hard rock. This rock represents the heart of someone with a hard heart. The water in this squirt gun represents some of the good stuff in life: relationships, education, risks, sports, clubs/activities. You will squirt the rock with the squirt gun several times. There are some people who are not open to learning or experiencing new things. They have a hard heart, and the water will not soak in. It just rolls off. Now hold up the sponge and have them list some properties of it. Explain that the sponge represents someone with a soft and open heart. Then squirt the sponge several times. When a person has a soft and open heart, they will soak in the information and opportunities. You can interchange *heart* and *mind* during the lesson, because it is just as important to have an open mind.

Discussion:

1. Are you more like the rock or the sponge?

2. Are you like a sponge sometimes and a rock at other times? What makes the difference between you being more like a rock/sponge?

3. When would it be okay for you to be more like a rock... not open to influence? (Peer pressure, etc.)

4. Are you prepared to learn?

5. What would it take for you to be like a sponge in school?

6. In what condition is your heart?

7. What are the advantages of being like a sponge?

8. What does it mean to be stubborn?

9. What are some reasons why people might be stubborn or close-minded?

10. How can you work with someone who is stubborn?

51 Made Smooth from the Rough Stuff

Topic: Perseverance, Dealing with difficult things in our lives

Materials: Types of sandpaper, pieces of wood

Time: 15 to 30 minutes.   **Space:** Classroom or outside area

Activity: This is a good activity to demonstrate how our struggles make us into better people. You will demonstrate how a piece of sandpaper is not too rough, but just rough enough to make a piece of wood smoother. Show the group a piece of wood and some sandpaper. Does anyone know what the purpose of sandpaper is? It can be used to rub the wood, making it smooth. I can even use the sandpaper to round off these edges. Ask for a volunteer to feel the sandpaper and describe how it feels. Ask the group, "If it is rough and scratchy, how can that sandpaper make a piece of wood smoother?" Use the sandpaper and rub one edge of the wood to round it off. Even though the sandpaper is rough, it is just rough enough make the wood smoother. The sandpaper is rough, but not too rough. It has the right texture to prepare the piece of wood.

Discussion:

1. The sandpaper is similar to the problems and difficulties we experience in life. We experience just the right amount that is needed to prepare us.

2. What are some examples of problems that people your age may go through that only make them stronger?

3. We have the amount of strength needed to get through these rough times and they are often needed to prepare us for the future. The rough times we experience help make us smooth so we can better handle our problems in the future. We become stronger and more mature.

4. Before wood can become a beautiful piece of furniture, it must be sanded by the rough stuff. Before we can become smooth, we must go through some rough stuff.

5. Do you agree that we need to go through tough times in our lives to get stronger?

6. What are some tough and rough times that people your age might go through?

Shawn Becker

52 *Stand the Test of Time*

Topic: Being strengthened by our experiences

Materials: Balloon, rock, dart

Time: 15 to 30 minutes.   **Space:** Classroom or outside area

Activity: This is a simple activity that shows how our life experiences shape us. It can also be used to show how we can withstand pressure if we are prepared for it. In this activity, the balloon will represent our lives that have not been developed, while the rock represents a life that is prepared for the circumstances it faces. You will take the balloon and explain that it represents someone who has given up, a person who has not learned from their mistakes, a person who cannot see any good coming from their own personal struggles. Hold the balloon up, along with a dart or pin in your other hand.

Explain that the pin represents trials, temptations, and struggles that an individual will face. Move the balloon closer to the dart as you ask the group, "What happens when we run into hardships that we are not prepared to handle?" If we are not strong enough, we will pop just like this balloon. Then hold the rock up with the dart. As you bring them close together, explain that we need to do things to strengthen our coping skills. We need to talk about our problems. We need to ask other people for help. We need to set goals and manage our time. We need to build positive, healthy relationships. We need to study and do our homework. We need to eat well and take time to relax. If we do these things, we will be strong enough to survive when we face hardships and difficult times.

Discussion:

1. What things can help us gain strength so we can better withstand life's trials?

2. What are some of the things people your age face that might try to "pop" you like the dart?

3. Have there been times when you have been popped like a balloon? What happened?

4. What are some good or positive things we can gain from going through struggles?

5. What can you do to make sure you are better prepared for the next dart that comes at you?

53   People Pencils

Topic: Being strengthened by our experiences

Materials: Pencils, pencil sharpener

Time: 15-20 minutes   **Space:** Classroom

Activity: This is a very easy lesson. All you need is a few pencils and a sharpener. Show a dull pencil to the group and ask what you can use it for if it is not sharpened. Then sharpen it and have the group explain what you can now use it for. We are all like pencils because the good stuff is in the middle. We often need to be "sharpened" by life experiences in order to be useful. Our life circumstances can bring out the best in us. The tough times that we go through can sharpen us so that we can be used in the future. Without those situations, we would be like a dull pencil.

Discussion:
1. What does it mean that we are like a pencil?
2. What are some good things that we have stored up inside of us?
3. What are some things that might "sharpen" us, releasing our potential?
4. What would happen if none of us were ever sharpened? We would have very limited use and would miss out on reaching our potential, much like a dull pencil. Sharp pencils have many uses and are full of opportunity and hope. Make sure you are always sharpening yourself.

54 What Pacifies You?

Topic: Finding happiness

Materials: A pacifier, string, markers

Time: 15 to 30 minutes.   **Space:** Classroom

Activity: You will need to tie strings to the pacifier before the activity. Attach little pieces of paper with different words on them to the strings. (Examples are: Nintendo, bike, I Pods, Cell phones, DVDs, CD's, different toys, etc.). When you are ready, hold the pacifier up to show the students. Keep the strings with the paper hidden in the palm of your hand. Ask the students what the pacifier is used for. The main use is to soothe the baby until you can get it some milk. Explain to them that's why they call it a pacifier. You might want to read them the definition of "pacifier." Then ask them, "What would happen if you gave it to the baby and never gave it milk?" They will answer, "It will die!"

Go on to explain that we often are using pacifiers. Hold up the pacifier so the strings can be seen. Read off the examples and say that people their age believe that if they had these things, their life would be wonderful. "If I only had that new Nintendo game, I'd be happy," "If I only had a new bike, I'd be happy," and so on. Explain to them that, "You would only be happy for a little while," reminding them of the definition of pacifier. The pacifier is a short-term solution. It only satisfies for a little while. The pacifier cannot keep us alive or happy. It wouldn't be long until we demand a new XBox game, bike, or whatever they want at the time.

Discussion:

1. What were some of the examples of pacifiers people your age ask for?
2. Why are these only temporary solutions?
3. What can happen if we set our happiness and survival on these pacifiers?
4. Do you think it is possible to be happy with just new games, bikes, phones?
5. What are some pacifiers that adults want?
6. What are the things that can really make us happy and truly keep us alive?
7. Were people happy before we had all the technology, toys, and gadgets we have now?
8. If we need these things to be *truly* happy, how could people have been happy before they had them?
9. What is *true* happiness? Where does it come from?

55   *Spoiled*

Topic: True happiness, Making choices, Values

Materials: Moldy bread, sandwich ingredients

Time: 20-30 minutes   **Space:** Classroom

Activity: You will be making a sandwich using at least one piece of moldy bread. Tell the group that you are very hungry and are going to make a nice sandwich. Start with a good piece of bread and then put your sandwich toppings on it. After you made your delicious sandwich, pick up one of the moldy pieces of bread to lay it on top. Make sure that you act very disgusted as you pick up and place the moldy piece of bread. Tell the group that you were looking forward to eating your sandwich but that you cannot eat it now. A little bit of mold ruined your entire sandwich. The same happens with us. Hanging around the wrong people, chasing the wrong goals, and making poor choices are all things that can cause mold in our lives.

Discussion:

1. What are some things that might cause "mold" in your lives?

2. Does mold grow quickly or slowly? It depends on the thing growing the mold, as well as the growing conditions. A piece of bread or fruit will mold more quickly during a hot summer week. Some of those things may cause you to mold more quickly because there will be "ideal" growing conditions.

3. What are some "ideal" growing conditions? (Peer group, addiction, lack of supervision, lack of values/goals/direction, free time, etc.)

4. Have you ever picked up a piece of bread or started to eat some food that you did not notice was moldy right away? Why did you miss the mold? There are times when it may be hidden on food so that we do not see it right away. We may even bite into it before we notice the mold.

5. Can this happen with people too? Can we have small amounts of mold on us that we do not detect right away? Why might people not notice the mold in their own lives?

6. A little bit of mold on a piece of bread can ruin the whole sandwich, just like a little bit of "mold" in our lives can ruin us.

7. What type of person can leave a bad taste in your mouth like mold does?

8. How can we make sure that we stay "fresh?"

56 Staying Centered

Topic: Remaining true to self, goals, friends, family

Materials: Lazy Susan, spices

Time: 20-30 minutes   **Space:** Classroom or larger space

Activity: You need a Lazy Susan or a turntable that goes in your cupboard for your spices. Demonstrate in some way how the things in the center spin much slower and don't fly off like the things on the outside. If you can't have the demonstration, then just have them picture the last time they were on a merry-go-round and have the class discuss what happens to a person in the dead center and what happens to someone on the edge when the merry-go-round is going very fast. If you have a merry-go-round, use it for the demonstration.

Discussion:

1. What do you think it means to stay centered?

2. At times life spins out of control. What can you do to make sure you do not go flying off as it spins?

3. How would this relate to your goals? There may be times when you need to stay focused on your goals even when they may be spinning out of your control.

4. How can this relate to your friends, family, or relationships? If you are centered on the right things, you won't lose control.

5. Being true to yourself can keep you centered. What does it mean to be true to yourself? You know who you are and what you value. You do not change.

57   Persuasion... Being a Follower

Topic: Following the crowd

Materials: Hairdryer, ping-pong balls

Time: 20-30 minutes   **Space:** Classroom

Activity: You can really WOW your group with this one. You will turn a hairdryer on and place a ping-pong ball on top of the air current. Here is the part that will WOW your group. Due to some scientific principle, the ball will hover above the dryer in the air current. It will stay hovering above, bouncing around on the current, even as you move the hairdryer around. You can even do a few tricks. Ask the group to predict what will happen before you perform the stunts. Try moving the hairdryer from side to side. The ball should stay up and follow the current. This can relate to us following our friends, teachers, or family. Then you can slowly tip the hairdryer to one side. The ball should stay up for quite a while before if falls off. For a good effect, you can tip the dryer so that the ball is just about to fall and then turn the dryer back up. Do this a few times, taking the ball right to the edge without dropping it. The point is that we are safe when we are being guided, but we will fall if we move too far away.

After you do a few fancy tricks keeping the ball up, explain that we are all like the ping-pong ball. We are kept up by and follow things that influence us. These things might be our families, friends, goals, or the media. Just like the ball, we all need something or someone to keep us up and right on track.

Discussion:

1. What are some of the sources of the air current in your lives? What or who pulls you in, keeps you up, or pushes you around?

2. Who are some people that you allow to influence you? Who do you follow?

3. What causes people to get off track and fall?

4. What causes good leaders to fall?

5. How do you know who or what to follow?

58 Backpack Burdens

Topic: Forgiveness, Grudges, Anger
Materials: Backpacks, books
Time: 20-30 minutes   **Space:** Classroom or larger space
Activity: You will need a big backpack and several books for this activity. Hold up the backpack and ask for a volunteer to come up and put it on. Give the person a book and ask them how long they could carry it around in the backpack before getting tired. Put the book in the backpack and ask the volunteer how they are doing. You will keep adding books, one at a time, to the backpack. When you add the book, give an example of a burden it might represent. Here are some examples: This book represents a fight you got into with your parents. This book represents your bike getting stolen from school. This book is your friend who started a rumor about you.

Check with the volunteer after each book is added to make sure there is not too much weight. Fill the backpack up with as many books as it can hold, so it is very heavy. Once it is full, ask the volunteer how long they could carry that backpack around now. Then ask the volunteer how long they could carry the backpack comfortably now. We all have heavy burdens that we carry around at different times in our lives. One burden that just weighs us down is holding a grudge. Holding a grudge does not help us in any way.

Discussion:
1. What did you notice as more books were added to the backpack?
2. What were your thoughts or reactions as I kept adding books?
3. Did it seem like our volunteer was under a lot of strain once the backpack was full?
4. What are some burdens that people your age carry around?
5. Do you know anybody who carries all their books to each class? There are students who carry around full backpacks everyday. What problems can that cause? What are some unnecessary burdens that we carry around?
6. Do you think that our volunteer reached their limit in how many books they could carry?
7. Do you think that people can reach their limits with the amount of burdens they can carry around?
8. How might we be able to tell if a person has reached their limit? How can we tell if an individual is under the strain of a lot of pressure?
9. What can we do when our burdens are piling up?
10. What can we do for other people to help them carry their burdens?

59   All Knotted Up

Topic: Trying to solve our problems all on our own

Materials: Pieces of string that are 2-3 feet long

Time: 20-30 minutes   **Space:** Classroom or larger space

Activity: This is a good activity to demonstrate how our problems can keep our energy tied up, especially if we do not get help. You will need to give everyone in the group a piece of the string. Once everyone has a piece of string, tell the group that they will have some time to think about the worries and stress they are experiencing. They should tie a loose knot on their string for each worry/stress that they have. You can give them about 5-7 minutes for this. After the time is up, have the group exchange their string with someone else.

This is symbolic of handing your worries/troubles over to someone else. Give the group a few minutes to untie the knots in the string they have received. Some people are better at solving other people's problems than they are at their own. After all the knots are out, they should return the strings to the original owner. We often keep our worries, fears, and stress tied up inside our bodies. We waste a lot of time and energy doing this, when what we really need to do is learn how to let go of them.

Discussion:
1. Why is it difficult for us to let go of our worries, stress, or problems?
2. What good does it do when we keep things tied up inside ourselves?
3. Some of us just keep going over and over things in our minds without taking action. What issues can this cause?
4. Do you know anyone who just keeps waiting for things to go wrong?
5. What does it mean to look for the worst-case scenario? Do you know people who always make things seem worse than they actually are?
6. What are some healthy ways we can let go of our worry or stress?
7. How can you help keep yourself and others from getting tied up with their worries?
8. Why is it hard for some people to let go of their worries and stress?
9. What difference would it make if we ask others for help when we feel stress?
10. Who are some people in your life that could help you with your problems?
11. Is it easy for you to ask others for help?

60   Left in the Dark

Topic: Feeling lonely

Materials: Large paper bags or blindfolds

Time: 20-30 minutes   **Space:** Classroom

Activity: Give everyone a paper bag or a blindfold. Then have kids scatter around the room and sit on the floor. Tell them that you want all of them to sit silently for three minutes with their bags over their heads/blindfolds on. This experience won't work unless everyone maintains perfect silence, so don't communicate with anyone in any way. Tell them when three minutes are up. You may also want to turn the lights off while they are blindfolded. After three minutes, call time and collect the paper bags/blindfolds.

Discussion:

1. How did you feel during this experience?
2. What was it like to be left in the dark? Have you ever felt like that before?
3. How was this experience like lonely times you've had? Explain.
4. How easy or difficult is it for you to be by yourself? Why?
5. What things do you usually do when you are feeling lonely?
6. What things can people do when they feel lonely?
7. Is it okay to be lonely at times?
8. What are some things that you need when you are feeling lonely?
9. What can you do for another person when they are feeling lonely?
10. Lonely times can be painful, but they can also be times when we really grow and become stronger.
11. What are some ways that loneliness can strengthen us?
12. In what ways can you grow when you are going through a lonely time?

61 Perspective Puzzle

Topic: Difficult experiences make us stronger and complete
Materials: Puzzle pieces
Time: 20-30 minutes   **Space:** Classroom
Activity: This is an activity that can demonstrate that we are shaped by our experiences. We have all had some very good things happen to us. Many of us also have lived through some terrible tough things. We need the good and bad experiences together because they help form a beautiful picture/person in us. You will need a puzzle that you will put together in front of the group. While you are putting the puzzle together, you will pick up a piece and say that it is very beautiful. Repeat this a few times. Then pick up a dark piece and say that it is ugly and that you do not want it in your puzzle. You will set this piece aside or throw it away. You will continue putting the puzzle together, alternating between some beautiful and ugly pieces. Make sure that you comment on the pieces as you either discard them or add them to the puzzle.

Some group member may raise the point that you cannot throw the "bad" pieces away. You need them to help form the picture in the puzzle. All the pieces are necessary to have a complete picture. All the pieces are necessary in order to form the beautiful picture in the puzzle. Not only are all the pieces needed to complete the puzzle, but also once the "ugly" pieces are added, they turn into part of the beautiful picture. If our lives were this puzzle, many of us would rather keep the ugly pieces out. We often complain when we are going through tough times. We want to only experience the fun and happy things. We get down and depressed and cannot see that the "ugly" pieces in our lives are also needed in order for us to be made beautiful. When we go through the bad stuff in our lives, it helps make us into complete and beautiful people.

Discussion:
1. What are some examples of beautiful things people experience?
2. What are some examples of tough or ugly things people your age have to deal with?
3. Tell me how a time like this can make you into a stronger person?
4. Why is it difficult to see these bad times in a more positive way?
5. Are we ever going to stop having "ugly" puzzle pieces in our lives? Why not?
6. Instead of just throwing them away, what can we change about ourselves, knowing that we will always have "ugly" pieces to put into our life puzzle?
7. Just like the "ugly" pieces were needed in the puzzle, we also need "ugly" pieces to complete our life puzzle. What does this mean?
8. What role does a positive perspective play in life?
9. Do you think that there are some people who focus only on the negative things that happen to them?
10. What difference would it make if we said that all the pieces were beautiful?
11. Do you think that we have more things go right in a day or wrong? Maybe you can keep a journal for a week to keep track. Many times we only focus on the "ugly" stuff when we have much more beautiful stuff surrounding us.

Shawn Becker

62 Emotion Responses

Topic: Healthy responses to situations that cause anger

Materials: Four clear glasses (three filled with water, one with vinegar), four spoons, baking soda, red food coloring, green food coloring, towel

Time: 30 minutes   **Space:** Classroom

Activity: You may want to try this one before you do it with your group so that you know how it will work. There is some set up that you need to do before the activity. You will need to place the glasses on top of the towel in the following order: Water, Water, Vinegar, Water. You will place a spoon with one or two drops of red food coloring covered with baking soda next to the first glass. (Don't use too much food coloring or it will "bleed" through.) Next to the second glass, you will have a spoon with one or two drops of green food coloring covered with baking soda. (Again, not too much food coloring.) You will have a spoon with just baking soda on it next to the third and fourth glasses. You want to make sure that each of the four spoons looks the same sitting next to the glasses.

Ask the group to think of a time when they got mad. Stir the "red" spoon into the first glass of water, while the group is thinking. Now have them think of a time when they were jealous. Stir the "green" spoon into the second glass, while they are thinking. Then ask them to think of a situation that made them "boiling" mad. Stir the third spoon, but be prepared because this one might get messy. Finally, ask the group to think of healthy appropriate ways to respond and deal with your negative feelings. As they are thinking about and listing these ways, stir the last spoon into the last glass. Make sure that you point out to the group that this was the cleanest one without any reactions.

Discussion:

1. What are some things that people your age do when they get "boiling mad?" These are things that may spill over and cause a mess like the third glass.

2. What does it mean to be green with envy?

3. What things make people your age jealous or envious?

4. What can we do to keep ourselves under control when we get mad or jealous?

5. We want to handle our negative feelings so that we end up like the fourth glass. There is no mess and the feelings are gone. What things do we need to do in order to make sure we deal with our feelings in healthy ways?

6. What are some examples of healthy ways to deal with anger or jealousy?

Educational Media Corporation®, Box 21311, Minneapolis, MN 55421-0311

63   Priorities

Topic: Priorities, Time management

Materials: A clear container about a quart in size, golf ball, corn/popcorn/soybean seeds

Time: 30 minutes   **Space:** Classroom

Activity: This is a good way to show how we need to set our priorities first so that we can work everything else in around them. Explain to the group that the jar represents our lives. We have many things that we try to fit into each day, but many days we run out of time. We need to organize our time so that we start with the most important activities we need to get done. Start pouring some of the seeds into the jar as you list some things that people in the group might do on any given day. If it is a school group, you might have a list like this: wake up, get dressed, eat breakfast, brush teeth, take the bus to school, stop at locker, go to first class, and so on. Keep going until the container is full. Once it is filled up, try fitting the golf ball in. You will not be able to make it fit. Have the group members think of something important that the golf ball can represent, something that really needs to get done that day. Maybe it is studying for a test. Maybe it is talking to a friend who is mad. As they can see, their day is already full, so there is no way they will get that thing done. That is what happens when we put off the important things.

Then you can dump the seeds back out of the container. You will pour a small layer of seeds to line the bottom of the container. Then place the golf ball in the middle of that layer and slowly add the remaining seeds. To their amazement, all the seeds will fit in the jar covering the golf ball. When we focus on our priorities and start with the important things, we will have enough time to get them done and enough space to fit them in.

Discussion:
1. Did you think that all the seeds would fit into the jar after the golf ball was put in?
2. Have you ever had your day fill up with things to do?
3. What are some important things that people your age put off doing?
4. What does this saying mean: "Don't put off until tomorrow what you can do today?"
5. What are the dangers of procrastination?
6. What problems can procrastination cause for students?
7. How do you set priorities? How do you know what you should do first?
8. What are the "golf balls" in your life that you need to put first?
9. Who is someone you know that is organized and has good priorities and time management?
10. What can you do to become more organized?
11. What can you change in order to manage your time better?

Personal Choices

64 Trash Cookies

Topic: Watch what you put into your bodies
Materials: Cookie jar, trash, cookies
Time: 20-30 minutes   **Space:** Classroom or larger space
Activity: This is an activity that demonstrates that what we put into our bodies will be what we get out of them. You need to have a cookie jar with some cookies to put in it. Ask the group what the jar is called. They will say that it is a cookie jar. Ask them what goes into a cookie jar. Of course it is cookies! If I put cookies into the cookie jar and you reach in, you should pull out a cookie. Now put some trash into the cookie jar. Ask them what they would pull out now if they reached in. Since it is still a cookie jar, they should pull out a cookie. Right?

We are like the cookie jars, because we hold whatever is put into us. We should make sure that we fill ourselves with good stuff. We should avoid filling ourselves with "trash." We should not hang around with bad people. We should not watch bad movies or television shows. We should not listen to "trashy" music. We need to be careful because what we put into our bodies is what will come out of them.

Discussion:
1. Would you eat a cookie from the cookie jar with the trash in it?
2. What if I took the trash out and then put the cookies back in? Why not?
3. Would you eat a cookie if I put it back into the jar after I cleaned it?
4. What are some good things that we put into our bodies, minds, and hearts?
5. Why is it important to fill our lives up with these things?
6. What are some examples of "trash" that we put into our bodies, minds, and hearts?
7. What can happen if we only put "trash" into our bodies, minds, and hearts?
8. Is it possible for us to be good while we are letting trash enter our lives?
9. If we are all like cookie jars, what do we need to do to clean ourselves inside?
10. What does it mean that we get out what we put in?
11. What can you change to reduce or eliminate the amount of "trash" you let into your body?

65 Garbage In Garbage Out

Topic: Things that influence our beliefs, actions, and feelings

Materials: Magazines, glue, scissors, pencils, large paper, markers

Time: 30-45 minutes   **Space:** Classroom

Activity: Each person is given a large piece of paper to draw their face in the center of it. Have the participants look through magazines to find pictures of things they are likely to see/hear/taste/touch/smell in an average day. These pictures are to be cut out and glued to their poster with an arrow pointing to how they get into our bodies/minds (i.e., eyes, ears, nose, hands, etc.).

Discussion:

1. Was it easy to find pictures of things we see, hear, touch, smell, or taste?
2. How do these things get into our bodies?
3. What are some examples of things that we see, hear, smell, taste, or touch that might be harmful to us?
4. What are the risks of letting harmful things into our minds and bodies?
5. How can we prevent the harmful things from getting into our minds and bodies?
6. What are some examples of healthy things we see, hear, touch, smell, and taste?
7. What can we do to expose ourselves to more of these healthy things?

66   Dyed Hands

Topic: Things that influence us

Materials: Bowls or cups, water, food coloring, paper towels

Time: 20 minutes   **Space:** Classroom

Activity: You will need to make up a jar or cup full of colored water the same as you would for coloring eggs. You can use hot water (not too hot) with a tablespoon of white vinegar and food coloring. Before you do the activity, let the group know that they will be getting dye on their hands that will take a few days to fade. Ask for volunteers who would be willing to put their fingers or hand into the jar with the dye. Have them put their fingers or hand into the dye and then dry off their hand. They will notice that they cannot wipe the dye off, no matter how hard they try.

Discussion:

1. We may not appreciate the capacity of our minds to absorb and remember if we think it doesn't matter what books, movies, or other activities are fed into it.

2. Our mind, like the dyer's hand, is colored by what it holds; that is, if I hold my hand in purple dye, my hand becomes purple.

3. It does not take long for your hands to get colored by the dye. The same is true for our minds and lives.

4. It does not take long for things we watch, listen to, or read to influence us.

5. What are some examples of things you do not want to "dye" your hands or minds with?

Shawn Becker

67   Dirty Laundry

Topic: Things that influence our beliefs, actions, and lives

Materials: Dirty socks, shirts, pants, bags

Time: 30-45 minutes   **Space:** Classroom

Activity: Take a sock (an old one, preferably one you don't care about getting muddy), soak the sock in mud, get it really dirty, and then put it in a plastic bag. Take it to your class and during your lesson ask someone if they would mind putting on a sock (of course they haven't seen the sock yet); someone will volunteer. Then take out the muddy sock from the bag and ask them to put it on their clean foot. Hopefully no one will want to do this. You can do this with other types of clothes, too. You can get a shirt and pair of pants all dirty, stained, and smelly. Tell them you have a new pair of clothes to give them. Ask for volunteers to wear the new clothes. You can also make up a pair of "new" socks for every person, or several people in your group. Ask them if they would like a new pair of socks and hand them out. Have them take off their shoes and socks. Pass out the bags with your "new" socks to the volunteers. Make sure they are in a bag so no one can see or smell them. Once everyone has the bag, tell them to put on their new socks.

Discussion:

1. Were any of you excited to get new clothes/socks?

2. Did you expect to get a dirty sock?

3. What was your reaction when you saw the sock?

4. Did any of you want to put the sock on after you saw it? Why not?

5. Can you put a dirty sock on your foot and expect it to feel okay?

6. What can happen if you put on the dirty sock? What would happen if you put the socks on and then put on your shoes?

7. Would any of you want to put a dirty sock inside of your shoes? Why not?

8. We would not cover ourselves with dirty clothes and expect to feel good. Yet we fill our insides with things that are not clean and we expect to feel good.

9. What are some unclean things that we fill ourselves with? (i.e., friends, jokes, movies, books, internet, attitudes, beliefs, foods)

10. How do these things get inside our bodies? (i.e., ears, eyes, etc.)

11. How can we control what things we let inside so that we remain clean and feel good?

68   Colorful Celery

Topic: How people influence us

Materials: Celery, glasses, water, food coloring

Time: 20 minutes and then several days   **Space:** Classroom

Activity: This object lesson will take several days. You will need to take at least one stalk of celery and split it up the center about halfway up the stalk. Once it is cut, you will stick one side into a glass with red-colored water and the other side in blue-colored water. You can check the celery every day, but it will take a few days for it to reach its full effect. After a few days, the celery stalk will draw up the colored water and the celery will be tinted red or blue.

You can also do this by placing several stalks of celery into the same glass with food coloring. It will slowly soak up the dye after a few days. If you had a few together, you can say it is like a group of friends who hang out together. The friends are all influenced, just like all the celery was.

Discussion:

1. See how easily this stalk of celery took on the color of water in which it was sitting. It only took a few days for the entire celery stalk to soak up the colored water. Can any of you think about how this might be related to people?

2. We are just like that stalk of celery. We "soak" up the characteristics of the people we spend time with. Our friends and families have a big influence on who we are.

3. How are your friends influencing you? What things are you "soaking" up from your friends?

4. Are they "colored" with anger, yelling, cheating, lying, peer pressure, sarcasm, and criticism?

5. Are your friends "colored" with patience, cooperation, soft-tones, kindness, honesty, and laughter?

6. You will reflect and become like the examples you receive from your friends. Since you take on the characteristics of the people you are around, it is important to ask yourself, who are your friends?

69   It's What's Inside that Counts

Topic: Character, Integrity

Materials: A variety of chocolate bars or chocolate kisses, a hollow chocolate candy bar

Time: 20 minutes and then several days   **Space:** Classroom

Activity: This activity is sure to be a favorite one, if you like chocolate. It has to do with what is inside of us. You will need to get a variety of chocolate bars for your group. Have some that are solid, some that are caramel or cream filled, and some that are hollow. You can use ones that have other stuff in them also, but you need to have the first three for sure.

You can start with the solid candy bar. Cut or break it open so that the group can see that it is pure and solid. Next, break open the filled candy bar and say that it looked like it would be solid. The filled candy bar can represent us. We look like we are pure and solid on the outside, when all we have is a layer of goodness.

Finally, cut or break open the hollow candy bar so that everyone can see that it is hollow. Not everything is as it appears. Tell them that this one looks like it is solid chocolate but it is not. We can be fooled by the way things look and by the way people look on the outside.

Discussion:
1. Were any of you fooled by the different candy bars? Did any of you think they were all solid?
2. Could you tell that they were not solid just by looking at them?
3. Can you tell what type of person someone is just by looking at him or her?
4. What do we need to do if we really want to see what a person is like inside?
5. What problems can occur if we try to guess what people are like without really getting to know them?
6. What do we need to do in order to become more solid and pure?

70   100% Pure

Topic: Things that influence us, Integrity

Materials: Orange juice, water, clear glasses

Time: 15-20 minutes   **Space:** Classroom

Activity: This activity demonstrates that we are influenced by others and may get watered down. You will need to have at least two glasses. You can have a volunteer from the group help you out. You will pour one glass full of orange juice. You will also need to pour a glass half-full with the juice. Have your volunteer taste the full glass of 100% pure juice and the half-full glass. Have them explain how the two taste. Now add some water to the half-full glass and do another taste test. Keep adding more water to the glass, tasting it after each addition. What you will find is that it will not taste as good as the 100% pure glass. We all start off like the glass of 100% pure orange juice. Many of us, though, end up getting watered down so that we have little purity left. We are watered down by our choices and the life experiences that we have.

Discussion:

1. What are examples of things that influence us and water us down?
2. What are some choices that young people make that decrease their purity?
3. Is it possible to maintain your purity? How?
4. If you do get watered down, can you get your purity back? How?
5. How can friends affect your purity?
6. How can the media, movies, TV, and music affect your purity?
7. Who are the most "pure" people you know?
8. What makes them "pure?"
9. Is it possible to be "100% pure?"
10. What do you need to do to become pure?
11. What can you do to protect your purity?

Shawn Becker

Additional resource books I enjoy and use

Cain, J. & Jolliff, B. (1998). *Teamwork and teamplay: A Guide to cooperative challenges, challenge and adventure activities that build confidence, cooperation, teamwork, creativity, trust, decisions making, conflict resolution, resource management, communication, effective feedback, and problem solving skills.* Dubuque, Iowa: Kendall/Hunt Publishing.
Website: www.teamworkandteamplay.com

Cavert, C. (1998). *Games & other stuff for group book 2.* Oklahoma City, OK: Wood & Barnes Publishing. Website: www.fundoing.com

Jackson, T. (1993). *Activities that teach.* Cedar City, UT: Red Rock Publishing. Website: www.activelearning.org

Jackson, T. (1995). *More activities that teach.* Cedar City, UT: Red Rock Publishing. Website: www.activelearning.org

Jackson, T. (2000). *Still more activities that teach.* Cedar City, UT: Red Rock Publishing. Website: www.activelearning.org

Olson, C. (2000). *Energizers: Calisthenics for the mind.* Minneapolis, MN: Educational Media Corporation.

Rohnke, K. & Butler, S. (1995). *Quicksilver: Adventure games, initiative problems, trust activities, and a guide to effective leadership.* Dubuque, IA: Kendall/Hunt Publishing. Website: www.karlrohnke.com

Schoel, J. & Maizell, R. (2002). *Exploring islands of healing: New perspectives on adventure based counseling.* Beverly, MA: Project Adventure. Website: www.pa.org

Sykes, S. (1995). *Feeding the zircon gorilla and other team building activities.* Tulsa, OK: Learning Unlimited Corporation. Website:www.learningunlimited.com

Sykes, S. (1998). *Executive marbles and other team building activities.* Tulsa, OK: Learning Unlimited Corporation. Website: www.learningunlimited.com

Sykes, S. (2003). *Raptor and other team building activities.* Tulsa, OK: Learning Unlimited Corporation. Website: www.learningunlimited.com